the perfect buzz

the perfect buzz

**THE ESSENTIAL GUIDE
TO BOOZING, BARS,
AND BAD BEHAVIOR**

HarperResource

An Imprint of HarperCollins*Publishers*

FIRST EDITION

Conceived, designed, and produced by

Quid Publishing

Level 4, Sheridan House

112-114 Western Road

Hove BN3 1DD England

www.quidpublishing.com

Publisher: Nigel Browning

Publishing Manager: Sophie Martin

Design: Lindsey Johns

Illustrations: Steven Bannister

Editorial: Ian Whitelaw

Additional research by International Barman and cocktail expert
Robert 'Martini' Brandt

Library of Congress Cataloging-in-Publication Data is available on request

ISBN 0-06-077970-5

05 06 07 08 09   10 9 8 7 6 5 4 3 2 1

contents

introduction

Ever since primitive man learned how to get the cork out of a wine bottle, mankind has, quite literally, been intoxicated with alcohol. Throughout history, alcohol has worn many faces and played a variety of roles around the globe. It was once viewed as the elixir of life and credited with great medicinal powers. Even today, alchemists mix it with ground gemstones to create potions that will stabilize your astral body. It has played an integral role in religious ceremonies and rituals throughout the ages, and has been enjoyed by everyone from Jesus to Homer Simpson. It has also helped destroy civilizations and been the target of religious fervor, leading to the historic, yet unsuccessful, Prohibition years in the US.

Perhaps alcohol's most significant role, particularly in today's society, however, is that of acceptable social lubricant. Taken in moderation, it has the power to loosen the tongue, raise the spirits, take the sharp edge off life, and heighten the libido. Overdo it with the devil's brew though, and you can expect to wake up with eyes like raisins, head like a volcano, and breath like Lassie. This book is not, however, here to pass judgement on where, why, or how much you drink, but to help you choose and know what to drink, be it organic ale, vintage wine, cool spirit, or good whiskey. And if that's not enough, by the end of the book you will not only be an expert on the wet stuff, but you should have enough bar trivia and tricks up your sleeve to keep you in free drinks the rest of your life!

CHEERS!

the wet stuff

lager & beer

past and present

IF PROSTITUTION IS THE WORLD'S OLDEST PROFESSION, THE BREWING OF BEER IS CERTAINLY ITS MOST ANCIENT FORM OF MANUFACTURING. A VITAL PART OF LIFE FOR MANY OF THE EARLIEST KNOWN CIVILIZATIONS (WHERE IT WAS REGULARLY INCORPORATED INTO DAILY WAGES), EVIDENCE OF BEER HAS BEEN FOUND EVERYWHERE FROM ANCIENT CHINA AND EGYPT TO THE INCA AND ASSYRIAN CULTURES. IN FACT, RECIPES FOR 19 DIFFERENT BEERS WERE RECENTLY DISCOVERED ON SUMERIAN TABLETS DATING BACK NEARLY 6,000 YEARS! EVER CONSIDERATE, THE EGYPTIANS EVEN PLACED BREAD AND BEER IN THE TOMBS OF THE DEAD TO TAKE WITH THEM TO THE AFTERLIFE (A RITUAL HOMER SIMPSON WOULD SURELY APPROVE OF).

For a long time beer was drunk through a straw, owing to the crude brewing techniques that left sediments of grain at the bottom of the cup. In Ancient Babylon, the king's straw, naturally, was made of gold, and was long enough to stretch from the throne to the nearest container of beer.

To the Romans, beer was nothing more than the drink of Barbarians, but this did nothing to stop its meteoric rise once Christianity had established itself throughout much of Europe. As with the development of wine, the monasteries played a large role in improving the brewing process. It was in the monks' interests to get it right; when fasting, they were entitled to drink as much of the stuff as they wanted, but all it took was one bad barrel and there'd be no hangover—just a room full of dead monks.

With the exception of monks and priests, up to the Middle Ages the brewing of beer was strictly a job for women, as it was considered a food as well as a celebratory drink. In fact, until the time of Britain's Queen Victoria, there were few taboos regarding women or even children drinking beer. Indeed, during the seventeenth century, schoolchildren in England were given two bottles of beer each day at school, Queen Elizabeth I drank strong ale each morning before breakfast (which perhaps explains why she never married), and ladies-in-waiting at the court of Henry VII were each allowed a gallon of beer per day.

Beer, like wine and champagne, has long been associated with rituals and festivities. One of the patron saints of brewing is none other than St Nicholas (a.k.a. Santa Claus), which perhaps accounts for his cheerful disposition, rosy complexion, and beer belly. In fact, the expression "Yuletide" is a derivative of "ale-tide," suggesting that the Christmas tradition of getting plastered is a time-honored ritual. Beer also has an interesting connection with weddings. In Ancient Egypt, the only proper gift to be offered to a pharaoh by a suitor seeking the hand of a princess was a keg of beer, while in Europe during the Middle Ages, brides often sold ale on their wedding day to help cover the expenses (a tradition now sadly lost)— hence the origins of the word bridal ("bride-ale").

When Columbus first reached North America, he found the native people had "a first rate brew, brewed with maize and resembling English beer." The first colonial settlers in Virginia were quick to follow suit, using corn to brew their beer, and it's a good thing they did, as the first shipment of beer from the old country did not arrive until 20 years later! It wasn't long before the colonists were placing ads in the London papers recruiting brewers, and the first known brewery in the New World was established in Manahattan in 1612.

By 1810, 132 breweries were serving 185,000 barrels of beer to a population of 7 million people, and as the population boomed over the next 60 years, so did the number of breweries, topping 4,000 in 1873 and producing 9 million barrels of beer for a population of 40 million.

Then things started going downhill. Price wars, mergers, Prohibition, a swelling temperance movement, wars, and high taxes reduced the number of breweries to just 230 by 1961. It was the microbreweries that came to the rescue—in the mid 1990s they were opening at the rate of at least three a week, and more than 1,500 breweries supply the discerning US drinker today.

All beer brewed and drunk around the world was ale (dark beer) until the 1830s, when the Germans isolated a strain of yeast that produced a lighter, more carbonated beer with a drier flavor. By the 1840s it was being brewed in the US, and nowadays light beer dominates US and world sales.

From the cozy pubs of England to the sweltering bars of Australia, beer remains the number one tipple throughout the whole of the Western World. Why? The answer is simple—at the end of a warm summer's afternoon, or even on a hostile winter's night, nothing beats an ice-cold beer. Cheers!

"WHERE BEER IS BREWED, THEY HAVE IT GOOD." CZECH PROVERB

the essentials

- Beer is made from barley malt (which gives the fullness to the flavor), hops (which add the bitterness), yeast (which converts the barley malt sugars to alcohol), and water (which acts as a medium during the fermentation process).

- The differences between types of beer come about through the brewing process, and are defined by the type of yeast used and the temperature at which fermentation takes place. Although barley has traditionally been used in most countries for fermentation, in recent years wheat beers have become a popular alternative.

Light Beer/Lager

A paler, drier brew with a smaller alcohol content, light beer, such as Budweiser, is bottom fermented, which means that the yeast falls to the bottom of the barrel, leading to a slow fermentation at a colder temperature and a higher degree of carbonation.

Dark Beer/Ale/Bitter

Higher in alcohol, more robust, and more complex than lager, English-style dark beer is top fermented. The yeast remains at the top of the barrel, allowing for rapid fermentation at a warmer temperature, creating a dark drink with a prominent head and a stronger hop flavor.

light beers (lagers)

GERMANY AND THE CZECH REPUBLIC
The undisputed number one light beer-brewing nation in the world has to be the Czech Republic—a country with a long reputation for being obsessed with beer and the art of brewing it. In fact, the Czechs got so drunk during the 1970s that they invited Frank Zappa to join their government, and their president was moved to write a play based on his experiences working in a brewery!

Although the name (and flavor) of Pilsner has been greatly used and abused by countless beer companies around the world, it is in fact named after the Czech town of Pilsen. In Germany, too, the Pilsner brewery has a reputation for excellent quality. If you can get your hands on the genuine article, Radeberger, Bitburger, Jever, Sparten, and Konig are all cracking brands with a crisp, malty flavor and heady quality. Another German specialty is Helles, a light, refreshing beer particularly favored in summer. Good brands of Helles include Löwenbrau and Hofbrau.

And finally, I can't mention German beer without including Budweiser Budvar. Bearing no relation in taste to American Budweiser, this beer is sweeter and less hoppy than Pilsner Other similarly excellent brands include Zamek and Sampson.

NORTH AMERICA

With a light beer history almost as long as that of Germany, the US can claim some expertise in the field, but most of the major brands are unexceptional. Sam Adams is probably the best of the widely-known brands, but if you want to try some really excellent US beer, you have to go to a decent bar that stocks beer produced by the local (or not so local) microbreweries. Particularly good examples include San Francisco's Anchor Steam (which has been made by Anchor Brewing for over 100 years), Hennepin from Brewery Ommegang in Cooperstown, NY, Baltimore Brewing Company's DeGroen's Weizen wheat beer and their Czech-style DeGroen's Pils, and Victory Prima Pils from the Victory Brewing Company, Downingtown PA. To sample them all might take a heroic Kerouac-style journey across the States, but I can think of worse ways to spend a summer…

BELGIUM

They may be ridiculed for being boring (try and think of a famous Belgian that isn't Hercules Poirot), but the Belgians certainly know how to make good beer. Stella is one of their better-known exports, but the one to seek out and spend the rest of your life thanking me for is Leffe. This really is a beer for the connoisseur, rich in flavor, heady, and one of my favorite tipples. Be warned though—the Belgians like their beers strong. Both Leffe Blond and Brown are around 6.5%!

AUSTRALIA

For a country that prides itself on its love of beer, Australia on the whole produces some pretty noxious, chemical tasting brews. Banging on about the importance of keeping it ice-cold is one thing, but, as the saying goes, you can't polish a turd. Best avoided. And English lager is no better.

> **FACT** OVER 30 BILLION GALLONS (114 BILLION LITRES) OF BEER IS DRUNK EACH YEAR THROUGHOUT THE WORLD.
>
> WORLD BOOK ENCYCLOPEDIA

dark beers

India Pale Ale (IPA)

IPA is a golden colored ale with a strong and distinctive hoppy flavor. Originally an export ale, it is currently undergoing a mini-revival in the US, which can only be a good thing. There are numerous breweries right across the United States currently brewing IPA, so your choice of a good bar will dictate the likelihood of finding the stuff. The cream of microbreweries include Catamount Christmas Ale (brewed in Vermont), Anchor Liberty Ale (CA), Vail Pale Ale and Solstice Ale (HubCap Brewery & Kitchen, TX), Sierra Nevada Celebration Ale and Renegade Red (High Country Brewing, CO), Blue Heron (Mendocino Brewing, CA and NY), and IPA (Rubicon Brewing, CA).

Wheat Beer

Very fashionable of late, wheat beer, or white beer, is exactly as the name suggests — a beer made from wheat. (And before you ask, despite its pale color, wheat beer is actually an ale, hence its inclusion in this section.) It is wonderfully refreshing and, for beer, is even a touch exotic, demanding as it does that a slice of lemon, orange, or even cucumber be thrown in to complement the flavor. The best stuff comes from Europe (try Belgian Hoegaarden, or Germany's Weissbräu), but US wheat beers such as Wit (Thomas Kemper, Seattle), Celis White (Michigan Brewing Co.), and Rubicon's own brew are also top-notch.

Bitters/Pale Ales

What England lacks in good light beers (lagers), it makes up for with its bitters and pale ales. In fact, on a cold, blustery night in winter, a good pint of bitter and a steak and kidney pie in an old English pub can be a religious experience.

The good stuff? Adnams, Timothy Taylor's, Young's Special, Spitfire, Flowers, Old Peculiar, London Pride, Fullers ESB, Bass, Burton, Royal Oak, Worthington White Shield, Whitbread Pale Ale, Samuel Smith, Marston's Pedigree Bitter… the list is endless. But to save putting up with English food, bad weather, and the trains, the US now produces some damn fine ales of its own. Recent award-winners include Pike Pale Ale (Seattle, WA), Pullman Pale Ale (Riverside Brewing, Riverside, CA), Holy Cow Pale Ale (Casino Cafe & Brewery, Las Vegas, NV), Burning River Ale (Great Lakes Brewing, Cleveland, Ohio), Doggie Style Ale (Flying Dog Brewpub, Aspen, CO), Pyramid Pale Ale

(Pyramid Breweries, Seattle, WA), and Gray Whale Ale (Pacific Coast Brewing, Oakland, CA). Again, find a good bar and good beer will follow…

Porter

Like wheat beer, this dark colored London ale is also experiencing something of a revival in the US. Outstanding brews include Blue Ridge Porter (Fredrick Brewing, Frederick, MD), and Point Reyes Porter (Marin Brewing, Larkspur, CA).

Brown Ale

Good US versions of this traditional English beer include Bristlecone Brown Ale (Uinta Brewing Company, Salt Lake City, UT), Bond Street Brown Ale (Deschutes Brewing, Bend, OR), Lazy Days (Yakima Brewing Co., Yakima, WA), and the invitingly named Moose Drool, (Big Sky Brewing Company, Missoula, MT).

But when all is said and done, the UK's Newcastle Brown Ale is still the original and the best.

TOP TEN MOST FAMOUS BEER DRINKERS

1 Homer Simpson and Barney (now sober)

2 Norm from Cheers

3 Benjamin Franklin

4 Al Bundy

5 Falstaff (Shakespeare)

6 John Belushi

7 Ernest Hemingway

8 ZZ Top

9 The City of Munich during Oktoberfest

10 Charlie Papazian (author: *The Joy of Home Brewing*)

stout & guinness

past and present

INSTANTLY RECOGNIZABLE, UNIQUE IN FLAVOR, A MEAL IN ITSELF, AND THE LIFEBLOOD OF IRISH CULTURE, GUINNESS AND THE EMERALD ISLE ARE AS INEXTRICABLY LINKED AS WOODY ALLEN AND HIS TRADEMARK GLASSES.

The story goes that in 1759, the now-legendary Arthur Guinness bought a dilapidated Dublin Brewery, which he leased for 9,000 years. (Guinness had either rather vain ideas of his own immortality, or incredible foresight.)

As well as traditional beer, Guinness also tried his hand at brewing "Porter," a dark beer, common in England but fairly new to Ireland. Taking its name from the porters of Covent Garden and Billingsgate markets, who lived off the stuff, Porter was unusually dark, owing to the fact that it was made from roasted barley. Guinness brewed this beer so well that he had soon ousted all English exports of the stuff. Within 30 years Guinness had come to totally dominate Ireland's brewing industry, had become the staple diet of every Irishman capable of staggering to the nearest pub, and was on its way to making a fair attempt at world domination.

Today Guinness is the most famous Irish drink in the world and is sunk in vast quantities wherever sold, from the dusty bars of Ireland to the ghastly Irish-themed pubs that span the world from New York to London. It continues to lead the advertising world with its innovative, thought-provoking adverts, and has almost single-handedly reinvented St Patrick's Day as a global holiday for idlers, drunkards, and layabouts. So let's raise our glasses to Guinness, and wear our white, foamy moustaches with pride.

HOW THE PERFECT PINT OF STOUT SHOULD BE SERVED

If you want a perfect pint of stout, ask for a "slow one." A good barman will appreciate this; pouring the perfect pint of stout is an operation that simply cannot be rushed—it is a three-stage process that should take a good couple of minutes if performed properly. Firstly the pint glass, tilted at about 43° (give or take a degree or two), is three-quarters filled. After being allowed to settle, the glass is then topped up and again allowed to settle. Finally (and if this happens, you should plant a big sloppy kiss on the barman's lips for being such a perfectionist), the excess head is trimmed off with a knife.

But it doesn't end there. If you're a true Guinness devotee, you'll wait a couple of minutes more for the drink to "settle." As Flaubert once said, "Anticipation is the most reliable form of pleasure."

GUINNESS MYTHS

You get a better pint in Ireland

Not true. The Guinness sold in North America is brewed in Ireland and made with the water from the Wicklow mountains, south of Dublin, and therefore exactly the same as the Guinness served in traditional Irish pubs. Of course it might not come served with a shamrock carved into the head, or to the accompaniment of fiddles and accordions, but then you can't have everything.

Guinness is black

Not true. It's actually the color of a very dark ruby. The next time you have one, hold it up to the sunlight.

Guinness is "good for you"

Guinness actually had to retract their famous "Guinness is good for you" advertisements on the grounds of misinformation (they cleverly retorted with "Guinnless isn't good for you!"), but it does contain iron and antioxidants, and has fewer calories than a pint of skimmed milk, so there is much to be said for its beneficial properties. And besides, as the saying goes, "if it feels so good, how can it be wrong?"

the essentials

Stout is the generic term for this unique type of dark beer (made of roasted, malted barley, hops, yeast, and water), of which Guinness is by far the best-known brand. It is brewed with soft water (like beer) but with top fermenting yeast (like dark beer), and it relies on very well roasted barley to give it its distinctive dark color and bitter taste.

- Bittersweet in flavor, a good stout should have hints of coffee and chocolate in the taste and a head of foam that lasts until the bottom of the glass.
- Stout tastes best on draught, second best from a can (with a widget), third best from a bottle.
- Guinness draught, first introduced to the US in 1967, is now one of the top selling imported draught beers.
- Guinness is the perfect accompaniment to steak, hamburgers, ribs, and most other beef or pork dishes. It also goes well with many desserts, such as dark chocolate cake and vanilla ice cream.
- Stout is also known in California as "big-boned beer."
- The best-known stouts are all brewed in Ireland.

other brands

BEAMISH With a darker, more burnt taste, Beamish is still brewed the closest to the original flavor of Porter, and for many lovers of stout (myself included) it is the superior one of the three best-known brands.

MURPHY'S Visually Murphy's is virtually indistinguishable from Guinness and Beamish, but is slightly sweeter in taste, with a hint of coffee and honey to its flavor—a well-balanced stout, though some would say a little lacking in character.

GUINNESS EXTRA COLD A bit gimmicky (especially in those bars with the tacky taps with the flashing lights). Guinness, to my mind, just doesn't benefit from being so cold—but I have a similar issue with iced coffee, so it's really all down to personal taste on this one.

vodka

past and present

IF IT'S PURITY YOU'RE AFTER IN A DRINK, LOOK NO FURTHER THAN VODKA. THIS CLEAN, COLORLESS SPIRIT HAS BEEN CHAMPIONED THE WORLD OVER, FINDING FAVOR THROUGH THE CENTURIES WITH SCANDINAVIANS, POLISH ROYALTY, RUSSIAN PROLETARIAT, SIBERIAN SHAMAN, AND—IN THE LAST 60 YEARS—JUST ABOUT EVERY BAR IN THE WESTERN HEMISPHERE.

Vodka is just the perfect all-rounder of spirits. It's the ideal partner for any mixer, can be flavored with just about anything imaginable and, unlike most other alcohol drinks, doesn't make your breath smell like a cross between cabbage soup and a gas-station when you've had a few. In its checkered history, vodka has even been applied as an after-shave in sixteenth-century Poland and used by Stalin as a means of suppressing revolution (by making vodka cheap and easily available, he effectively—and deliberately—reduced the entire country to a state of endemic inebriation). But while vodka's success can't be disputed, its origins can. In fact, this is still a thorny subject amongst the Poles and Russians, who would rather eat their own dogs than concede to the notion that vodka originated anywhere but their own backyard (the evidence, however, leans in favor of Poland).

Being such a pure spirit, water quality is of the essence in making good vodka and, like many early drinks, vodka was at first flavored to hide its unpleasant taste. In 1780, however, a chemist, hired by the Russian czar to make the drink more hygienic, developed a technique for purifying vodka by filtering it through charcoal, making it far more palatable and pure. (Unsurprisingly, the Poles also claim this invention as their own, but let's not go there.)

Despite the Cold War, vodka really took off in the US in the 1940s, thanks largely to the clever ploys of Smirnoff, who marketed their drink as a cool, pure, clean spirit—"a white whiskey"—and it became the mixer of choice throughout the cocktail era. It was the easy way that vodka accepts any mixer that made it such a hit. Just add a little ginger beer and "Voilà!," you have a Moscow Mule.

In the 1980s, Absolut upped the ante by introducing the idea of vodka as a shooter, something that, until then, had been unthinkable. From then on, it's been plain sailing, with flavored vodkas now a fashionable (though far from original) way of spicing up the rather neutral flavor. Sharp, clean, adaptable, cool, with a good alcoholic hit, it's no surprise that vodka remains such an easy, undemanding, and stylish drink.

the essentials

Vodka is a pure spirit, diluted with water and filtered before being bottled. It can be produced from anything containing starch or sugar: molasses, barley, maize, rye, millet, wheat, and potatoes. A good starched shirt will not, however, make very good vodka.

- Vodka originated in Poland, Russia, and Scandinavia during the fifteenth century, and it remains the national drink in all three areas to this day.
- The Eastern European word vodka translates as "little water," an alchemical idea of the spirit as elixir.
- As a rule of thumb, Western vodkas tend to be fairly neutral, while those produced in Eastern Europe have more of a distinct flavor and character.

FLAVORED VODKAS

Flavors have been added to vodka since day one, though this practice has became extremely fashionable of late, with countless bars selling bottles of vodka flavored with everything from sweets to bison sweat. The true connoisseur should be wary of gimmicks (many are often just flavored with essences) and stick with the classics, such as tatra (herbs), limmonaya (lemon peel), pierprzowska (chilli pepper), krupnik (honey and herbs), or wisniowska (sweet cherry).

How To Infuse Your Own Vodka:

1. Take an empty vodka bottle.

2. Choose your flavorings. Melon, butterscotch, chilli, apple, cinnamon, and vanilla all work well, but if you feel like throwing caution to the wind, why not make up your own bizarre combinations such as rhubarb and garlic, or beetroot and honey?

3. If using pieces of chocolate or toffee, always break them into smaller parts before adding—they will break down more easily.

4. Place your flavoring and the vodka in the bottle.

5. Add sugar to sweeten.

6. Replace the lid and leave for two or three days

7. Shake regularly (the bottle, not yourself).

8. Serve chilled.

brands

ABSOLUT

One of the coolest brands on the planet, Absolut has done more for vodka's renewed popularity worldwide than all the competition put together, and it finally put Sweden on the map for producing more than just Abba. Of the many special flavors, Citron, Kurant, and Mandarin really hit the spot, while Absolut Peppar is the essential Bloody Mary mixer, searing the throat like a burning coal. Nice.

FINLANDIA

Another Scandinavian triumph—uber-cool and a smart choice as a shooter or mixer. Be careful with the flavors though—they can be a bit hit and miss. The cranberry is too sweet and not dry enough (for my taste), though the Finlandia Lime hits the mark with its cool, zesty flavor and peppery kick.

SMIRNOFF RED

The brand that broke the US, Smirnoff nowadays seems a little old-fashioned, and it has certainly been superseded by many other smarter, purer brands. A touch medicinal in flavor, Smirnoff works best as a mixer (it makes a good Screwdriver and Bloody Mary), though some Russians will tell you the only thing it's good for is rubbing into your veins on a cold night.

GREY GOOSE

Although wholly US owned, Grey Goose vodka is produced in the Cognac region of France, under the watchful eye of a master distiller. A five-step distillation process and blending with water from the famous champage limestone Gente Springs gives Grey Goose the clean, crisp taste that recently earnt it 96 out of 100 points from the Beverage Tasting Institute, and the only platinum medal. It was also the winner of the prestigious World Spirits Championship. Now one of the fastest growing brands in the US, the company has recently added La Vanille to a flock that includes L'Orange and Le Citron as well as the original Grey Goose.

WYBOROWA

Inexpensive but superior quality Polish vodka, made from rye. Having a smooth, satisfying flavor with a hint of toffee, Wyborowa certainly lives up to its name (it is Polish for "exquisite") and attracts strong loyalty amongst its aficionados.

HOW TO MAKE THE PERFECT BLOODY MARY

- 2 ounces good vodka
- Dash red wine
- Pinch celery salt
- Salt and pepper
- 7 drops Worcestershire sauce
- 1 container organic tomato juice
- Celery stalks
- Cherry tomato

Mix well in a highball glass containing ice and serve with a celery stick and cherry tomato.

gin

past and present

FOR SUCH A SEEMINGLY INNOCENT AND SIMPLE DRINK, THE HISTORY OF GIN READS LIKE THE PLOT OF SOME FANTASTIC NOVEL. THE RASPUTIN OF SPIRITS, IT HAS SERVED AS A LIFESAVER, INSPIRED RIOTS, CAUSED DRAMATIC RISES IN MORTALITY RATES, AND RISEN FROM THE GUTTER TO THE HEIGHT OF SOPHISTICATION.

Gin first came about in the seventeenth century, when thousands of Dutch settlers, desperate to get away from all those tulips, windmills, and hard cheeses, headed for the East Indies. Upon arrival, however, they got more than they bargained for, in the form of tropical fever and kidney complaints. To their rescue came Dutch medical professor Dr Franciscus Sylvius, who invented Genever, later to become known as gin (though Dutch gin still goes under this name)—a simple combination of pure alcohol and juniper berries, that acted as a cure-all for the unhappy ex-pats, owing to the diuretic properties of juniper.

Gin's popularity soon spread to the UK, thanks to King William III, who cynically plied it to his troops fighting in Holland, knowing that they'd be more willing to sacrifice themselves to king and country if in a state of fine inebriation—hence the origins of the phrase "Dutch Courage."

By the eighteenth century, half the population of England was guzzling the stuff. Owing to the combination of gin's cheapness, the plethora of back street gin distilleries, and the unsavory things found floating in the drinking water, the average man, woman, and child in London was consuming over two pints of gin per week! For nearly a hundred years the entire population of London was blind drunk. Mortality rates soared. Business was good for undertakers, but gin was bad for business. Once christened "Mother's Milk," gin earned a new nickname, and "Mother's Ruin" was denounced as a curse of the poor and uneducated.

> " OF ALL THE GIN JOINTS IN ALL THE TOWNS IN ALL THE WORLD, SHE WALKS INTO MINE. "
>
> HUMPHREY BOGART, CASABLANCA

Its reversal of fortunes a mere 30 years later is therefore rather miraculous. Having proliferated during Prohibition, after the successful exportation of the cocktail party from the UK, there was no stopping it: gin became the drink of fashion. Its subtle flavors made it easy to mix, giving rise to such classic cocktails as the Martini (gin and vermouth) and Tom Collins (gin, soda water, sugar syrup, and lemon juice).

By the 1960s the tide had turned again. No longer the tipple of the young and fashionable, gin's associations with the bourgeoisie meant that Bob Dylan was not to be spotted sipping Martinis, and the Velvet Underground were not writing lyrics about "heading up to Lexington 125 to buy a gin and tonic." But, like a good dog, such a characterful spirit as gin can't be kept down. With public tastes demanding more purity in their drinks, and the rise in popularity of new brands such as Bombay Sapphire and Absolut, gin is back with a bang.

GIN AND TONIC

Of course, no discussion on gin would be complete without the mention of the good old "G&T." As with gin itself, this classic drink came about for medicinal purposes. Quinine in tonic water was used to fight off malaria, but was thought of as such an unpalatable drink that is was mixed with gin to make it bearable. To get the equivalent dosage of a modern anti-malarial drug you'd now have to drink several gallons of G&T.

One such advocate of gin and tonic, who indeed drank several thousand gallons in his lifetime, was Monty Python's Graham Chapman, who remained permanently drunk on G&T for the whole of the 1970s. A drinking companion of Keith Moon of The Who, the two set themselves pretty high standards when it came to the level of alcohol consumption the human body could withstand. Chapman, being a qualified doctor, diligently worked out the exact number of G&Ts required to kill a man and drank one glass less per day! Although the two successfully went through detox together, in order to work together on a film project (The Odd Job Man), both men died prematurely from their drinking habits, although it must be said that during their brief but intense time on Planet Earth, neither ever contracted malaria.

the essentials

- While any flavored spirit over 37.5% can be called gin, distilled gin is the combination of juniper and other botanicals macerated in neutral spirit, distilled in a copper pot, and mixed with water.
- Good quality gins can contain up to 20 botanicals, including coriander, angelica, liquorice, almond, and cinnamon.
- Pink gin is created by the addition of Angostura (an aromatic bitter bark).
- The best gins are 40% proof or above. Any lower than this should be strictly avoided.
- Gin should, ideally, be stored in a fridge. or even a freezer.

SLOE GIN

This traditional winter drink is made by infusing gin with the flavor of sloes—small purple-blue wild plums from the blackthorn bush. It is said that if the sloes and sugar are added to the gin at Halloween, the sweet, rich drink will be ready for Christmas, but it tastes far better a year later. Once the tipple of English Victorian ladies, sloe gin now adds color to a range of funky cocktails.

styles and brands

BOMBAY SAPPHIRE

This world-class gin belongs to the London Dry family. Originally taking its name from the unsweetened gin made by the middle-class London distillers in the late 1800s, London Dry is now made as far afield as Málaga in Spain. Beefeater and Gordon's remain the best-sellers of this style, but Bombay Sapphire has a far finer flavor—tasting the way freshly mowed grass smells—as well as a very desirable blue bottle.

TANQUERAY MALACCA

As well as a popular London Dry gin, Tanqueray also offer their Malacca gin. Named after a city in Malaysia, Malacca has a rich, characterful flavor better suited to drinking straight or on the rocks than mixed (if you can appreciate gin straight). The juniper flavor is obvious, but there is a complex underlay of other spices, including cloves, and a sweet aftertaste, very different to most other styles of gin. Definitely not something you'd find in your dad's drinks cabinet, and a gin that puritans may turn their noses up at, Tanqueray Malacca is a bold, adventurous drink that the more spirited drinker will revel in.

PLYMOUTH GIN

Still made in Plymouth, England, by one age-old distillery, Plymouth Gin is richer than London Dry, less dry, and has a wonderful heather and lavender aroma to it—one of the best gins on the market and reasonably-priced.

CITADELLE GIN

Not as widely available as the other gins mentioned above, Citadelle is a real curio, well worth seeking out, especially for gin aficionados. Its unusual bitter-sweet flavor, with a hint of oranges, derives from an eighteenth-century French recipe and, like Tanqueray Malacca, it is a gin that should not be wasted on mixers but drunk on its own. No water. No ice. Just gin.

bourbon/
tennessee whiskey

past and present

THE ROCK AND ROLL OF SPIRITS, BOURBON'S REPUTATION AS A HARD LIQUOR FOR HARD MEN REMAINS UNDISPUTED, EVEN TODAY. FOR HARD-BOILED WRITERS, LOOSE WOMEN, AND KEITH RICHARDS, A BOTTLE OF JD AND A FAG REMAIN THE STATUS SYMBOL FOR THE LIFE OF EXCESS. IT'S SURPRISING THEN THAT THIS NOTORIOUS SPIRIT ORIGINATED IN KENTUCKY, WHERE THREE QUARTERS OF ITS COUNTIES TODAY ARE ACTUALLY "DRY."

The production of whiskey in Kentucky first began in the 1700s, when the Scots and Irish immigrants found that the most profitable venture for their excess grain was to distill it (not only is whiskey easier to transport but also, unlike flour, it improves with age). At that time it would, of course, have been little better than moonshine (with a taste not dissimilar to floor polish)—until, that is, the legendary Reverend Elijah Craig "discovered" the burnt barrel method of aging whiskey that we now know as bourbon.

In one version of the story, Elijah—a fire and brimstone Baptist with a sideline in distilling whiskey—deliberately burnt a barrel to disguise the smell of fish that had previously been stored in it. Another story recounts that it was simply left on the fire too long by accident, while one account even claims that the process was dictated to the Reverend in a dream by a disembodied voice calling himself Keef. Whatever the case, the effect darkened the whiskey, and the natural sugars released from the wood added a caramel and vanilla-like sweetness to the spirit. While drinking the stuff would undoubtedly have still been a fairly joyless, sour, teeth-sucking experience, this was instantly recognized as a superior drink, and it became an overnight success.

Although the whiskey industry ended up in a fairly sorry state after Prohibition and World War II, the growth in demand for high-quality premium spirits in Japan during the 1980s helped revive the popularity of bourbon worldwide, leading to its undisputed position today as the drink of choice (if a little clichéd) for all wild-living guitar-wielding miscreants.

JACK DANIELS

Generally thought of as the US' favorite bourbon, Jack Daniels isn't strictly bourbon at all, as part of the distilling process involves filtering the liquid through maple charcoal, thus defining it not as a bourbon but as Tennessee Whiskey. It is interesting to note that the famous Mr Daniels began distilling at the tender age of 7, and by the time he was 13 was already running his own distillery! Jack's life came to a suitably rock-and-roll ending in 1911 after complications arising from a broken toe. The breakage was the result of one of his infamous temper tantrums when, furious that he couldn't open his safe, Jack gave it a damn good kicking.

JD MYTHS
(as perpetuated by the brand)

Jack Daniel's nephew Lem Motlow is still the proprietor.
He isn't: he died in 1947.

Lynchburg, where the company is based, has a population of just 361.
It hasn't: the current population is actually 5,740.

the essentials

- Bourbon can be made anywhere in the US, but only Kentucky bourbon may advertise the state where it is made.
- Proper bourbon is made from a minimum of 51% corn, to which is usually added a percentage of small grain, such as rye, barley, and wheat. It is distilled and stored in charred new white oak barrels for a minimum of two years.
- If bourbon is aged for anything less than four years (and I recommend you steer clear of any that are), this must be stated on the label.
- The final flavor of bourbon is determined not only by the varying degrees of the grain but also by the position of the barrel in the warehouse, the temperature variations, and even the color of the warehouse itself—with black, brown, cream, and red currently being the most popular hues!
- Bourbon was used as a cure for snakebites in the nineteenth century, two pints being the standard dose.

> " **BEANS AND BOURBON.**
>
> **AN EXPLOSIVE COMBINATION.** "
>
> STAR TREK'S CAPTAIN JAMES T. KIRK

brands

MAKER'S MARK

The absence of rye in Maker's Mark makes it an altogether lighter, softer ride than most other bourbons, and an excellent starter for the novice bourbon drinker (i.e. it won't burn holes in your teeth), at a price that won't break the bank.

JACK DANIELS

Although it has never marketed itself as a rock-and-roll drink, Jack Daniels is still synonymous with rebellion. Beyond the cool image, however, Jack Daniels is a rather inferior whiskey: overpriced and coarse in flavor. Those in the know should go for the far superior Gentleman Jack, JD's elder, wiser, and more sophisticated brother.

BOOKER'S

The bad boy of bourbon, Booker's is completely uncut and unfiltered, and it clocks in at 126% proof, meaning it'll put hairs on your chest before you've even taken the cap off. Dangerously good, reliably expensive, and surprisingly smooth. Just don't go spitting it on your campfire.

WOODFORD RESERVE

One of the best bourbons around, this is currently the author's favorite tipple. Elegantly packaged, and with a light, unobtrusive flavor, Woodford Reserve flows over the tongue and down the hatch like honey. For such a smooth, all-rounded flavor, this bourbon's value for money is hard to beat.

BASIL HAYDEN'S

Part of the "Small Batch Bourbon" line produced by the Jim Beam Distillery, this is aged longer than standard bourbons (such as Jim Beam White) and is of a higher proof. Strong, smooth, exquisite—Basil Hayden's is well worth the money if you feel like treating yourself to something special.

HOW TO MAKE THE PERFECT MANHATTAN

- **2 ounces good rye or bourbon whiskey**
- **½ ounce sweet vermouth**
- **1 dash of Angostura bitters**

Stir with ice.

Strain into a cocktail glass.

whiskey

past and present

WHISKEY (OR WHISKY, IF IT'S PRODUCED IN SCOTLAND, CANADA, OR JAPAN) TAKES ITS NAME FROM THE OLD GAELIC PHRASE "UISGE BEATHA," MEANING WATER OF LIFE. IT IS A SPIRIT INEXTRICABLY LINKED WITH THE CULTURAL HERITAGE OF THE HIGHLANDS OF SCOTLAND, THE GREEN ROLLING HILLS OF IRELAND AND—MORE RECENTLY—THE SOUTHERN STATES OF THE US. IT HAS BEEN USED EXTENSIVELY AS A MEDICINE AGAINST COLDS AND FLU; FUELLED DANCING, RITUALS, AND CELEBRATIONS; HELPED DROWN MANY A SORROW AND NUMBED THE HARDSHIPS OF LIFE FOR COUNTLESS PEOPLE OVER THE CENTURIES. IT ALSO GOES DOWN GREAT WITH COKE, ICE, WATER, LEMONADE, GINGER BEER, AND EVEN COFFEE.

Like vodka, the origins of whiskey have been the subject of fierce dispute over the centuries. Although the Scots and the Irish both claim to have discovered it first, their evidence would hardly stand up in a court of law. According to the Scots, whiskey distillation first began in Scotland over 500 years ago, as "proven" by a rather spurious historical "receipt" that suggests that a certain Scottish friar, John Corr, had orders to deliver 400 bottles to the king of England (who was planning a serious night in with the boys). Irish legend, on the other hand, decrees that it was St Patrick who first brought whiskey to Ireland when he arrived there from France in the fifth century. As St Patrick is said to have been a Scottish immigrant, the Scots might seem the obvious winners, but there is a good deal of evidence to suggest that the art of whiskey distilling is as likely to have originated in the Middle East, or even China, as the British Isles, and certainly earlier than the fifteenth century.

After the dissolution of the monasteries in Scotland during the 1600s, whiskey production became a more domestic art, practiced (and sold) by apothecaries, surgeons, and even barbers, all of whom were thought to have mystical powers of healing. The fact that the Scots came to associate the regenerative powers of alchemy with a "short back and sides" probably says a lot about the amount of whiskey they were knocking back at the time.

Although Ireland's story is a similar one, during the nineteenth century the rise of Ireland's temperance movement—led by an evangelical killjoy named Father Matthew—resulted in over a third of Ireland's drinking outlets being closed (they've been making up for it ever since) and a huge slump in whiskey production. With the potato famine that followed, and Prohibition in the US not long after, the Irish whiskey industry took a hard battering for over 100 years. Nowadays just two companies, Jameson's and Bushmill's, dominate the market for whiskey from the Emerald Isle, but with the rise in popularity around the globe of "Irish" pubs, this is now the fastest growing whiskey category in the world.

Recent years have seen a further rise in global whiskey production in Asia. Japan has, of late, been producing some rather fine whiskies, some of which are up there with the best Scotch and Irish. India, China, and Thailand, however, have a long way to go—their whiskeys are still best confined to the kitchen cupboard and marked "domestic cleaning fluid."

the essentials

Beer fermented from grain is distilled to make whiskey.

Key factors affecting a whiskey's flavor are:

WATER Water forms such a large percentage of the final drink it is inevitable that its source plays a role (albeit small) in the final flavor.

GRAIN Rye, barley, and corn each give whiskey a different taste. When several grains are combined in the distillation process, this is known as a mash.

AGING Whiskey is aged in oak barrels. The type of oak, the length of the aging, and even temperature, play a vital role in the final essence of the drink. In fact, more flavor is imparted in this part of the process than in any other—hence the importance given to the age of a whiskey.

BLENDING Even single malt whiskeys are usually blended from different barrels, giving a unique flavor to each brand.

GLOSSARY OF TERMS

Single, Double, Triple
Describes whiskey made at one, two, or three distilleries.

Blend
Whiskey made from a combination of several whiskeys of varying ages, alcohol content, and water. If combined skillfully, a "blend" will have as pure a flavor as a "straight" whiskey, and often with a better and fuller flavor.

Malt whiskey
Whiskey whose raw material is only barley malt.

Scotch
Whiskey that is matured in Scotland and usually double or single distilled. A true "Scotch" is made with moss-water and malted barley dried over a peat fire, which accounts for its unique flavor.

Irish whiskey
Whiskey that, unlike Scotch, is triple distilled and not peated. Its reputation as having a coarse flavor, fit only for making Irish coffee, is a little unfair: being lighter and smoother than Scotch, a good Irish whiskey can taste very refined.

Sour-mash whiskey
A balance of rye and barley, usually defined as Bourbon or Tennessee whiskey (though they are produced very differently).

Canadian whisky
A unique whiskey produced from a wide range of grains (corn being the most important, though it is rye that usually contributes most of the flavor).

brands

GLENFIDDICH
Roughly translated from the Gaelic, Glenfiddich means "valley of the deer"—a suitably evocative name for the site of a distillery set amid forest in the heart of the Scottish Highlands. This single malt is available in a variety of styles, the excellent pine-and-peat 12-year-old Special Reserve being the most obvious starting point.

If you have a fat wallet and a very discerning palate, the Glenfiddich Rare Collection 1937, laid down at the time of the coronation of King George VI, should be on your must-drink list. It is said to be truly remarkable.

JAMESON'S
Triple-distilled Irish whiskey, and the world's number-one best-seller to boot, Jameson's is inexpensive, but with a smooth, soft flavor and a delicate hint of sherry—a good introduction to the delights of Irish whiskey for the novice.

JOHNNIE WALKER
An excellent Scotch, available in three classic "colors."
Black: The original and best, 12 years matured, rich, elegant, and fruity—a good all-rounder.
Red: Put on the market as a "lighter" option to Black. While viewed as a benchmark blend by some whisky enthusiasts, the Black remains superior in just about every way.
Green: A 15-year malt with a deep, nutty flavor. When the pay-rise comes, you'll know it's time to switch from Black to Green.

FAMOUS GROUSE

A popular choice for whisky-lovers, and for good reason—this classic Scotch bursts with flavor, from the initial nutty, vanilla hit to the aftertaste of chocolate and raisins. Another modestly-priced whisky and one of the best blends on the market.

BLACK BUSH

Also known as Bushmill's Liquor, this full-bodied, spicy, and smooth whiskey is triple distilled from malted barley and blended with a single grain. Excellent value for money and—originating from Ireland's oldest distillery—the embodiment of the true spirit of the Emerald Isle. If money is no object, the 16-year malt is sublime.

YOICHI SINGLE CASK WHISKY

For the open-minded whisky-lover, sampling a few of Japan's brands can be a pleasant surprise. Yoichi remains the best of the bunch to date and is a complex, peaty whisky available as a 10-, 12-, and 15 year-old. After seeing the fabulous *Lost in Translation*, however, to me Japanese whisky will always be inextricably linked with Bill Murray's sardonic expression as he raises just one eyebrow during the whisky commercial.

> " **ALWAYS CARRY A LARGE FLAGON OF WHISKEY IN CASE OF SNAKEBITE AND FURTHERMORE ALWAYS CARRY A SMALL SNAKE.** "
>
> ACTOR / COMEDIAN W.C. FIELDS

> " **WHAT WHISKEY WILL NOT CURE, THERE IS NO CURE FOR.** "
>
> IRISH PROVERB

> " **WHISKEY IS BY FAR THE MOST POPULAR OF ALL REMEDIES THAT WON'T CURE A COLD.** "
>
> DOCTOR'S PROVERB

rum

past and present

LIFE IN THE NAVY, SO THE SAYING GOES, IS "ALL SODOMY, LASHES, AND RUM," BUT IF ASSOCIATIONS WITH BUGGERY, WHIPPING, AND TATTOOED SAILORS AREN'T ENOUGH TO BLIGHT THE NAME OF THIS DARK, OILY DRINK, ITS ROLE IN THE SLAVE TRADE SHOULD. TO FULLY APPRECIATE THE TRUE HISTORY OF RUM, HOWEVER, IS TO KNOW THE HISTORY OF SUGAR.

Although sugar cane originated in Asia, its synonymy with the Caribbean began in the fifteenth century when Spanish and Portuguese settlers—more than a touch annoyed that there was no gold to be found—discovered that the islands had an ideal climate for growing sugar cane. As well as molasses and crystals, an early form of rum, appropriately named "Killdevil," was soon being produced from the cane. The name came about partly due to its "strong and unpleasant flavor," but also from the fact that if you drank too much of the stuff, it was touch and go as to whether you'd wake up with an almighty hangover or simply not wake up at all.

By the late 1660s, Killdevil had been rebranded and renamed ("rum," from the word "rumbullion," meaning uproar), and was being successfully exported to the American colonies. By the eighteenth century, it had overtaken gin as the preferred tipple of the middle classes. In fact, such was the rising demand in Europe and the colonies for sugar and rum that the notorious "slave triangle" was created. Rum, exported from New England, was sold in Africa in exchange for slaves. These slaves were then taken to the Caribbean to work on the sugar cane plantations to produce rum to be sent to New England for exportation. The consequences of this vicious circle of exploitation are still with us today.

By the 1700s, rum had also become the drink of choice of the British Navy, partly owing to the fact that beer and wine soon went off in the tropical heat. For 300 years, one of the rituals of naval life was the daily consumption of half a pint of grog (half rum, half water) until 1969, when it was finally replaced with tea and biscuits. With such a dark and troubled history, it's perhaps no surprise that in the last 80 years rum has suffered from an image problem in the US, with sales declining in favor of whiskey. In contrast, however, the growth in popularity of white rum has been spectacular. Since its creation in 1878 by Don Facunado Bacardi, this pale, delicately flavored rum has been giving vodka a good run for its money as one of the most popular mixers. Bacardi, in fact, has become so synonymous with white rum that nowadays most people are prone to ask for Bacardi and coke in a bar as opposed to white rum and coke—a situation that all other brands of spirit can still only dream of.

the essentials

Rum is produced from sugar cane, which is boiled, forming a crystallized residue and congealed dark mass (molasses). This is then separated from the sugar crystals, reboiled, and mixed with water and yeast. This mixture is then allowed to ferment, before being distilled and then set to age in oak casks for several years.

While virtually every major island group in the Caribbean produces its own distinct flavor, rum can be broadly categorized into three types:

Dark Rum
Produced in Jamaica, Haiti, and Martinique, dark rum is usually aged for 3-12 years, with the extra addition of caramel to create that rich, full-bodied flavor.

Light/White Rum
Aged for just one to four years, light rum has a much more subtle flavor, making it an ideal mixer. It is usually produced in the southern Caribbean islands, such as Puerto Rico and Trinidad.

Golden Rum
Produced mainly in Barbados, golden rum sits somewhere between light and dark in flavor and tone.

HOW TO MAKE THE PERFECT LONG ISLAND ICE TEA

- ½ **ounce vodka**
- ½ **ounce gin**
- ½ **ounce white rum**
- ½ **ounce Cointreau**
- **1 ounce lemon juice**
- **Splash of Cola**

Pour all ingredients into an ice tea glass, top with cola, and garnish with a lemon wedge.

styles and brands

BACARDI
Neutral and unexceptional, Bacardi is pretty much like most other cheap white rums on the market—apart from the advertising.

UK
The Brits still seem to like their rum cloying, treacly, and black. Given half the chance they'd make the stuff so thick you could turn the glass upside down and it would stay glued to the bottom. That isn't to say it's bad stuff, far from it: if you like it dark and sweet, the aged rums from Cadenhead and Bristol are superb.

CUBA
As well as making good music and fine cigars, the Cubans know a thing or two about rum. Havana Club is one of their finest brands. The Silver Dry is a light, delicate white that knocks the spots off Bacardi, the Seven Year is a sly, smooth, heavy duty dark rum (think Samuel L. Jackson in *Pulp Fiction*), while the 15-year is simply heavenly.

BARBADOS
While sounding like bizarre sex toys, Cockspur and Mount Gay are both top-class exports from Barbados. Dark, mellow, and smooth, with an aroma of butterscotch, they are two of the most drinkable rums on the market, and work equally well as mixers or simply to be sipped and savored on their own.

GUYANA
These guys are massive rum producers, making full-flavored blended rums for the US, British, and German markets. El Dorado is one of their best—it has a highly complex and satisfying flavor and is superb.

JAMAICA
For those who like their rums robust and strong, Jamaica remains a stalwart in this department, still producing a huge range of dark rums from the definitive Overproof to the dusty flavor of Appleton Estate.

VIRGIN ISLANDS
The sun-drenched island of St Croix is currently home to one of the most fashionable (and award-winning) rums of the moment: Cruzan Single Barrel Estate Rum. Taste it and it's easy to see why. Dry and medium-bodied, it has a complex array of flavors, from pecan and vanilla to smoky oak and tobacco. I'm normally wary of drinks that are hyped up, but this one deserves all the praise being thrown at it. It's not cheap, but it is sensational to taste, and should be drunk on its own, preferably on a tropical island. A word of warning: be prepared for a battle pulling the plastic cork out!

brandy & cognac

BRANDY: "A cordial composed of one part thunder and lightning, one part remorse, two parts bloody murder, one part death-hell-and-the-grave and four parts clarified Satan." Ambrose Bierce, from *The Devil's Dictionary*.

past and present

LEGEND DECREES THAT DURING THE SIXTEENTH CENTURY, A KNIGHT OF THE COGNAC REGION OF FRANCE MURDERED HIS UNFAITHFUL WIFE AND THEN, FOR GOOD MEASURE, BEHEADED HER LOVER. THE NEXT DAY, FEARING DIVINE RECRIMINATION (AND IN ACCORD WITH LOCAL SUPERSTITION), THE KNIGHT "BURNT HIS WINE" AND LEFT IT IN THE CELLAR. FIVE YEARS ON, HAVING LONG FORGOTTEN ABOUT HIS MISDEEDS, HE INVITED A FRIEND OVER FOR A BARBECUE, DUG OUT THIS MYSTERIOUS BOTTLE, AND THE TWO GOT DRUNK ON THIS UNUSUAL BREW. WORD OF THIS NEW SPIRIT SPREAD QUICKLY, AND SOON EVERYONE IN FRANCE WAS USING THIS METHOD (DISTILLATION) TO TURN POOR ACIDIC WINE INTO "COGNAC." AND SO BRANDY WAS BORN.

The truth, alas, is a little more prosaic. The Cognac region of France actually got off to a very late start in the history of this spirit. Brandy was being drunk socially in Spain and Italy in the thirteenth century, but it was another 400 years before the white wine of the Cognac region was discovered to produce an excellent brandy. However, once it found favor with the French aristocracy, brandy became one of France's most profitable exports. Cognac remains today the home of the world's most famous and premier brands.

Like so many other elixirs of its time, brandy was believed to be a cure-all, particularly in England, where even today it is administered for shock or exposure, despite medical evidence to the contrary. The classic image of the St Bernard dog, with a small barrel of brandy round its neck, running to the rescue of a mountain climber is unfortunate. Alcohol is the worst thing to

"AN AMERICAN MONKEY AFTER GETTING DRUNK ON BRANDY WOULD NEVER TOUCH IT AGAIN, AND THUS IS MUCH WISER THAN MOST MEN." CHARLES DARWIN

give to someone suffering from hypothermia, as it fools the body into thinking it is warm and lowers the body temperature even further. And, as Dr Watson once wryly pointed out to Sherlock Holmes in the story of *The Engineer's Thumb*, when a person is in shock, "they need a calming sedative, not a shot of alcohol!"

Brandy has long been seen as the pinnacle of spirits. When rum and bourbon producers wish to emphasize the quality of their brands, they will often say "comparable to a fine brandy." Despite this, it has never quite been able to throw off its stuffy image, a throwback to the days when it was the drink of choice of the bourgeoisie. It is, however, a drink that speaks of refinement, good taste, and maturity, and if it's a noble, dignified tipple you're after, cognac remains the king of drinks.

the essentials

- To make brandy, the raw ingredients (usually grape juice, although plums, apples, blackberries, apricots, and cherries may also be used) are fermented and turned into wine, which is then distilled.
- The name originates from the European word "brand," meaning "to burn."
- Brandy has a system all of its own to distinguish the different types. C: Cognac. E: Extra. F: Fine. O: Old. P: Pale. S: Special. V: Very Special.
- **Napoleon:** a brandy that is at least four years old.
- **Vintage:** the liquor is kept in a wooden cask until the time it is bottled.
- **Hors d'Age:** the exact age of the brandy is unknown.
- **Eau-de-Vie:** French term for brandy.
- **Applejack:** US brandy distilled from cider.
- **Armagnac:** fine brandy from the French province of Gascony.
- **Grappa:** Italian brandy made from wine pomade.
- **Slivovitz:** plum-flavored brandy produced in the Balkan countries.
- **Blanche:** clear brandy that has not been cask matured.

brands

Rather than going by name, it is much simpler and more reliable to choose a brandy by designation and then price. Quite simply, the more you pay, the better the product will be. The following list is on a sliding scale of quality.

FRENCH COGNAC

For the very best cognac (which will cost you an arm, a leg, and plenty more), go for bottles produced around Angouleme, north of the Dordogne, and aged in casks of Limousin oak. Remy VS Grand Cru and Courvoisier VSOP Exclusif are both excellent.

FRENCH ARMAGNAC

Established brands such as Janneau Tradition are very good.

FRENCH CALVADOS

If it's fruit brandy you're after, avoid the 3-Star and choose Hors d'Age standard; these are wonderfully dry.

SPANISH BRANDY

Fundador is a good, reliable brand.

ITALIAN GRAPPA

Avoid cheap grappa at all costs— it tastes like firewater. You have to pay through the nose for a good grappa, but you won't be disappointed.

SOUTH AFRICAN

KWV 10 is probably the best around at present.

tequila

Q Why did the Mexican push his wife off a cliff?

A Tequila!

past and present

TEQUILA'S ORIGINS LIE WITH THE AZTEC PEOPLES OF MEXICO, WHO MADE A BEVERAGE FROM THE AGAVE PLANT LONG BEFORE THE SPANIARDS ARRIVED IN A VILLAGE CALLED TEQUILA IN THE SHADE OF A DORMANT VOLCANO (ALSO NAMED TEQUILA).

When the Spanish conquistadors arrived in 1530, they were running out of brandy brought along from Spain, so they fermented the sugary agave juice. The first tequila factory was not established until 1600, when Don Pedro Sanchez de Tagle, the Marquis de Altamira, started to cultivate agave and distil tequila.

Tequila's reputation is as much a legend as it is an image problem. In movies, it was associated with dark, hot little adobe cantinas, and drunken cowboys with itchy trigger fingers. In real life, it has been famous around the world for its monumental hangovers. And, despite all this, many bars list tequila with their fine sipping brandies and liqueurs, and gourmet chefs use tequila to perk up even their most proven recipes.

Tequila is a spirit entrenched in myth. It is not hallucinogenic, and nor is it Mexican moonshine. Although some US brands stick a grub in their bottle, real Tequila does not have a maggot or any other worm in the bottle, and it's not made from cactus. It is, however, different from all the other liquors. It can exhibit the same complex subtleties as cognac, generate the same loyalty and passion as a fine wine, and stimulate good conversation and fellowship like a good whiskey.

There is a wrong and right way to drink tequila. The right way is to drink it slowly with a slice of lemon and salt. Put salt on the back of your hand, suck it, and then take a sip of tequila. Follow this with a small bite of lemon. The wrong way to drink tequila is to do "slammers," unless your idea of a good night out is spending it on your hands and knees crawling around the washroom wishing you were dead. Hence the old saying, "One tequila, two tequila, three tequila, floor."

the essentials

- From uptown restaurants to downtown clubs, from snifter sippers to margarita aficionados, tequila is "it." But with so many brands, more new bottles, and some hard-to-pronounce names, it can be tricky to know which tequila to choose—unless you know what to look for.

- Agave (pronounced "ah-GAH-vay") is the family of plants used to produce mezcal and tequila. It is found exclusively in the Jalisco area of Mexico. Only the distilled spirit of the blue agave plant is used for premium tequila. The best tequila comes from 100% pure blue agave rested or aged in oak barrels. All 100% Agave tequilas must be bottled in Mexico, so look for "imported" on the label.

- Norma Official Mexicana de Calidad is the official seal of quality. There are only a handful of officially recognized tequila distilleries in Mexico, and each is assigned a NOM #. Every tequila brand should carry a single, consistent NOM #. This assures you that brand of tequila has come from the same quality ingredients and process as the rest of the line.

The flavor and smoothness of each tequila is determined by the quality of its ingredients and the aging process it has undergone.

Tequila has four age classifications:

BLANCO (SILVER)
Clear unaged tequila, fresh and fruity, and closest to the taste of agave itself.

JOVEN (GOLD)
Unaged tequila with added cane sugar or caramel, slightly sweeter than Blancos, and having a distinctive golden color.

REPOSADO (RESTED)
Aged for at least two months in wood barrels, mellower than Blancos or Jovens.

AÑEJO (AGED)
The highest quality option, aged for at least one year in oak barrels—the choice for the most discriminating consumer.

brands

CHINACO BLANCO
This is the brand that started the luxury tequila boomlet in the US back in 1983, and the only one made in the eastern state of Tamaulipas. The entire line is superb and highly distinctive, with a particularly rich, filled-in quality to the body, but it's the blanco that provides the most impressive "peacock tail" of flavors.

EL TESORO SILVER
You can't get much more back-to-basics than this family-owned distillery, yet its tequilas—grown in the Los Altos highlands of Jalisco—have a refined, high-note aromatic character, while packing an array of pungent flavors that more than hold their own in any margarita.

SAUZA TRES GENERACIONES PLATA
Sauza's top-of-the-line silver, produced using a triple distilled process, is a big-bodied tequila with a clean, fresh, almost minty, herbal character. It's smooth enough to sip on its own, but its essential agave flavors are amplified rather than damped-down, making it an obvious premium cocktail choice.

HERRADURA REPOSADO
The company that invented lightly aged reposado tequilas still makes a knockout. Eleven months in oak gives the tequila a measure of balance without overshadowing its herb and tropical melon fresh agave character.

EL PATRÓN AÑEJO
Produced, like El Tesoro, in the Los Altos region, this aged tequila does exactly what añejo fans love. Supersmooth, with a mild sensation of sweetness, El Patrón Añejo is a seductive sipping drink.

DEL MAGUEY MEZCAL SANTO DOMINGO ALBARRADAS
This very limited-production line of single-village mescals may provide the most astonishingly complex, lingering sips of spirits you've ever tasted. Made from the related agave espadín and bottled at 98.4% proof, this version was originally distilled in a pueblo 8,500 feet above sea level in the southern state of Oaxaca. It wafts a kaleidoscopic range of spice, tropical fruit, and herb aromas that will knock you off your chair before you venture the first slurp.

JOSE CUERVO ESPECIAL
Jose Cuervo has conquered the world with its unique premium gold tequila, a distinctive blend of Reposado and other high-quality aged Cuervo tequilas. Jose Cuervo Especial is exceptionally smooth, with a hint of sweetness and a rich, well-balanced character of oak, spice, and vanilla tones.

cointreau

pat and present

THE MOST POPULAR AND BEST KNOWN OF ALL FRUIT-FLAVORED LIQUEURS, COINTREAU IS A DRINK THAT EVOKES VISIONS OF WARM TROPICAL COASTS AND LINGERING SUNSETS. IT SHOULD BE DRUNK—IDEALLY—WHILST WEARING A LINEN SUIT AND A PANAMA HAT, SITTING CLOSE TO A BEACH IN A SMOKY BAR WITH A CREAKY OLD CEILING FAN AND A FEW GNARLED OLD GENTLEMEN IN THE CORNER PLAYING CRIBBAGE.

The distilling firm of Cointreau was set up in 1849 by two former confectioners, Adolphe and Edouard-Jean Cointreau. Although their liqueur—a brand new spirit created from the fruits of the local area—was an instant success, it was very different to the Cointreau flavor we know today. It was in fact Edouard-Jean's son, Edouard, who had the vision of creating a crystal clear liqueur blended with citrus peels from exotic parts of the world. Of course, this may have just been an excuse to do some serious globe-trotting on his father's expense account, but the result—a smooth, strong liqueur with a bitter-sweet aftertaste—was an instant success. A man of vision, Edouard also knew a thing or two about packaging. Aware that the opaque bottles used by other distilleries were falling out of fashion, Edouard designed for Cointreau a distinguished amber bottle with rounded shoulders and a red ribbon logo. For over 150 years now, neither Cointreau's flavor nor its packaging has changed, and it remains an authentic choice of many top bartenders—delicious when drunk straight, over ice, or mixed with fruit juices, tonic, or lemonade, and essential for such classic cocktail recipes as the Side Car and the Mai Thai.

"I HAVE SEARCHED PASSIONATELY FOR THE QUINTESSENTIAL FLAVOR OF COINTREAU; I WANTED TO COMBINE CRYSTAL CLEAR PURITY WITH THE SUBTLETY OF TASTES OBTAINED FROM THE PERFECT HARMONY OF SWEET AND BITTER ORANGE PEELS. "

EDOUARD COINTREAU

the essentials

Cointreau is made from the bitter oranges of Haiti, Brazil, and Spain, and sweet oranges from the south of France. The fresh, sweet peels are macerated in neutral alcohol and distilled in red copper pots before being adjusted with refined sugar and water to create a smooth, warming flavor with the lingering afterglow of both bitter and sweet oranges.

vermouth

past and present

Once the epitome of cool, vermouth (the essential mixer for a Martini) has been championed by everyone from Winston Churchill to James Bond and Frank Sinatra. From the cocktail era to the swinging '50s, this was a drink no self-respecting hipster would have been without. The name Vermouth derives from one of its key ingredients—wormwood (also used in the preparation of absinthe). Wermut, the German for wormwood, was later Gallicized to vermout, and somewhere down the line an "h" was thrown in for good measure. While aromatized wines date back as far as Greek and Roman times, the origins of vermouth as we know it date back to the eighteenth century, though things really took off in 1863 with the birth of Martini and Rossi, still the world's biggest producers.

Like its close companion gin, vermouth was initially used as an elixir for good health. Only in the last 100 years has its role been demoted to that of aperitif and, later, a mere mixer. In fact, its status sank so low that at one point serious Martini drinkers would request for the vermouth to just be waved over the gin so that just its fumes diffused into the cocktail (the most fervent connoisseurs would just pass a photo of the bottle over the glass). But with chic cocktails back in vogue, this heady and herbal aromatic drink really deserves to be reappraised and, at the very least, to be reinstated as the aperitif of choice.

the essentials

- Vermouth is defined as an aromatized wine, meaning that it is fortified with spirit and flavored with different herbs and spices (including cloves, nutmeg, and coriander).
- Vermouth comes in three flavors: dry white (Extra Dry), sweet white (Bianco), and red (Rosso).
- Vermouth should ideally be drunk within three to four weeks of opening, as, being based on wine, it can oxidize.

There are two broad categories of vermouth:

Southern French—the most complex of all styles, exemplified by Noilly Prat.

Italian—lighter in flavor and exemplified by Martini and Cinzano.

VERMOUTH THE MOVIE THE ONLY APERITIF TO BOAST A STARRING ROLE IN A HOLLYWOOD MOVIE, VERMOUTH WAS THE SUBJECT OF THE 1966 FILM *THE SECRET OF SANTA VICTORIA*, WITH ANTHONY QUINN. SET IN THE HOMETOWN OF CINZANO IN ITALY, THIS FILM—BASED ON A TRUE STORY—FOLLOWS THE EXPLOITS OF THE TOWN'S CITIZENS DURING NAZI OCCUPATION, AS THEY RISK THEIR LIVES HIDING THEIR PRODUCE FROM THE OCCUPYING FORCES.

brands

NOILLY PRAT (pronounced nwa-yee prah)

Noilly Prat is very much designed as a mixer—it complements other flavors extremely well and is the essential vermouth for making a Dry Martini cocktail. Although some may find it a touch too sour to be drunk on its own, Noilly Prat is far more sophisticated and complex than its Italian counterparts. Put it this way—if Martini and Noilly Prat were people, I would rather be stuck in a lift with Martini, but I'd prefer to be entertained by Noilly Prat.

MARTINI & ROSSO AND CINZANO

While lighter and less multifarious in flavor than Noilly Prat, these two classic Italian vermouths both have a wonderfully delicate flavor, are sweeter, and work well not only as mixers but as drinks on their own, straight or on the rocks. Both brands are available as Bianco, Extra Dry, and Rosso.

HOW TO MAKE THE PERFECT DRY MARTINI

- Prechill the gin, shaker, and glasses in the freezer (vermouth should be chilled in a refrigerator).
- Pour the gin into a shaker of cracked ice.
- Allow the gin to 'settle' with the ice.
- Add the vermouth.
- Shake until shaker is frosted but not so long that your hand permanently freezes to the side.
- Pour in your glass.
- Casually introduce an olive.

NB. The ratio of gin to vermouth in Dry Martini can vary greatly, depending on exactly how "dry" you like it. This is, of course, purely a matter of taste, and will develop and change with time. A standard Dry Martini is usually made with a ratio of 8:1 gin to vermouth. A "wet" Martini should have a ration of 4:1 gin to vermouth. For a bone-dry Martini, a 12:1 ratio should do the trick.

absinthe

past and present

ALTHOUGH CREATED IN 1792 BY DR PIERRE ORDINAIRE AS A "VIRTUOUS BREW," ABSINTHE WAS, AND REMAINS, A DRINK OF INCREDIBLE STRENGTH (GOOD ABSINTHE SHOULD BE ABOUT 70% VOLUME!). A NOXIOUS GREEN BREW THAT RESEMBLES WASHING-UP LIQUID AND TASTES NOT UNLIKE COUGH MEDICINE, IT BECAME THE DRINK OF CHOICE DURING THE NINETEENTH CENTURY AMONGST THE BOHEMIAN AND ARTISTIC COMMUNITIES OF EUROPE, MOST NOTABLY THE PARISIAN CAFÉ CULTURE. NICKNAMED "THE GREEN FAIRY," IT WAS CHAMPIONED BY DEGAS, MANET, VAN GOGH, RIMBUAD, AND EVEN PICASSO, WHO PAINTED THE ABSINTHE DRINKER AND CREATED A BRONZE SCULPTURE, GLASS OF ABSINTHE, IN ITS HONOR. ONE OF ABSINTHE'S MORE RECENT DEVOTEES WAS ERNEST HEMINGWAY, WHO REGULARLY GOT THROUGH BOTTLES OF THE STUFF, EVEN AFTER IT WAS MADE ILLEGAL IN MOST PARTS OF THE WORLD. REFERENCES TO ABSINTHE APPEAR IN MANY OF HEMINGWAY'S FAMOUS STORIES, INCLUDING *DEATH IN THE AFTERNOON* AND *FOR WHOM THE BELL TOLLS*.

Much of absinthe's glamor comes from the preparation ritual and exotic blend of herbs used to create its unique taste, including wormwood, which, if taken in large enough quantities, is capable of inducing madness.

Indeed, at the turn of the twentieth century, absinthe was deemed such a harmful and toxic brew that it was banned from France and other sensible parts of Europe and was replaced with the more innocuous pastis, better known in the US as either Ricard or Pernod.

Having made a recent comeback, thanks to the pretensions of a few louche pop stars and artists, absinthe is now freely available again. Not quite the original bad boy it once was, absinthe has now had some of its strength and original active ingredients reduced or removed. (The "real" stuff is only available in little shacks up in the hills of the Czech Republic.)

To drink absinthe correctly, get a spoon of brown sugar, dip it in the spirit, light it, allow the sugar to melt, put the flaming sugar into the glass of spirit and—while stirring— pour in water to douse the flame.

After only a few glasses you will slowly be rendered numb from the legs up and, if you drink enough of the stuff, temporarily amnesic. Which brings to mind that old W.C. Fields joke, when, during one of his films, he rushes into his local bar early one morning with a worried look on his face, and says to the barman:

"HEY CHARLIE, DID I SPEND $20 IN HERE LAST NIGHT?"

"YES," THE BARMAN REPLIES.

"OH, THANK GOD FOR THAT," REPLIES FIELDS,

"I THOUGHT I'D LOST IT."

the essentials

- Like gin, absinthe is basically flavored vodka. The key ingredient, wormwood, is macerated in ethanol alcohol with various other herbs and spices to create the drink's unique flavor.
- Originally, the emerald green color of absinthe was due to the presence of chlorophyll from some of the plants used. Nowadays other ingredients (and colorings) are used to recreate the translucent hue.
- The active ingredient of absinthe has been identified as thujone (also an active component of marijuana), which is believed to account for absinthe's hallucinatory properties. Connoisseurs tend to favor brands with a high level of thujone.

"AFTER THE FIRST GLASS YOU SEE THINGS AS YOU WISH THEY WERE. AFTER THE SECOND, YOU SEE THINGS AS THEY ARE NOT. FINALLY, YOU SEE THINGS AS THEY REALLY ARE, AND THAT IS THE MOST HORRIBLE THING IN THE WORLD. "

OSCAR WILDE

THERE ARE TWO BASIC STYLES OF ABSINTHE:

French Still banned in its country of origin, French absinthe has a strong aniseed flavor and deep green hue. If served with water, real French absinthe should change color and turn cloudy, owing to the presence of antimony chloride in the ingredients.

Czech Spelt "absinth," this version of the drink is much bluer in color, with a more subtle flavor than its French counterpart. It does not turn cloudy when water is added.

Absinthe Friends

Should any budding artists be reading this and be contemplating the switch to absinthe in homage to its many talented and famous advocates, it is worth remembering that not only did Ernest Hemingway, a regular imbiber of this mind-altering brew, eventually commit suicide, but Vincent Van Gogh actually cut off the lower half of his left ear and gave it to a prostitute, when under the influence. When asked why he cut off his ear, Van Gogh is said to have famously replied, "I don't need to hear to paint!" Welcome to the strange and frightening world of absinthe. Drive carefully.

brands

LA FÉE
The only brand to be endorsed by Marie-Claude Delahaye (the curator of the absinthe museum in Paris), La Fée has a clean, fresh, strong aniseed flavor with hints of mint, lemon, and coriander. It is, for my money, the best absinthe currently on the market, and it is still made from the traditional wormwood recipe (though not in such strong dosages as to induce hallucinations and madness). And that spooky "eye" on the bottle actually belongs to Sarah Nixey, the singer of the band Black Box Recorder.

HILL'S
This is the best-known of the Czech brands and, at 70% ABV, adding water to a glass of Hill's is pretty much essential if you value your brain cells. Rediscovered by Jesus and Mary Chain guitarist John Moore, while on tour in Czechoslovakia, Hill's became a fashionable drink in London throughout the 1990s, and was instrumental in re-popularizing absinthe worldwide. Hill's has a pleasant enough taste, especially when poured over sugar or mixed with caramel, although, having such low traces of thujone, it is not quite the genuine article.

ABSENTA MARI MAYANS ABSINTHE
Though not as widely available as Hill's and La Fée, Absenta Mari Mayans is well worth hunting down: it is an excellent French absinthe, with a full, rich flavor and high enough thujone content to keep even the most hardened absinthe drinkers happy (and high). Impressive, too, is the fact that when water is added, not only does the drink turn cloudy, but it also foams in a rather spectacular way, bringing to mind the kind of alchemical brews drunk by mad scientists in old 1950s horror films!

drambuie

past and present

TOGETHER WITH WHISKY, HAGGIS, AND BILLY CONNOLLY, DRAMBUIE IS ONE OF SCOTLAND'S FINEST EXPORTS. TAKING ITS NAME FROM THE OLD GAELIC PHRASE "AN DRAM BUIDHEACH" (THE DRINK THAT SATISFIES), DRAMBUIE'S TASTE REFERS BACK TO THE DAYS WHEN WHISKY DISTILLERS IN SCOTLAND WOULD THROW IN AROMATIC PLANTS AND HONEY TO SWEETEN AND TAKE THE ROUGH EDGE OFF THE FLAVOR OF THEIR WHISKIES. THE SECRET RECIPE FOR DRAMBUIE HAS REMAINED WITH THE MACKINNON FAMILY FOR OVER 250 YEARS, SUPPOSEDLY GIVEN TO THEM AS A GIFT BY BONNIE PRINCE CHARLIE WHILE HE WAS HIDING IN SCOTLAND AS A CUNNING PLAN TO AVOID BEING CAPTURED.

It seems a fanciful idea that the usurped crown of England would have had the knowledge (or the time) for a spot of home-brewing, when half of England's army was out for his blood, but we'll let it pass as it's a good yarn. Whatever the case, the recipe has remained a secret within the MacKinnon family and, in keeping with tradition, only the women in the family are permitted to make the secret herbal infusion that gives Drambuie its unique flavor.

Comparable to Southern Comfort in many ways, Drambuie is a strong, earthy drink with an adventurous and maverick edge. For those who like an element of danger with their cocktails, mix it in equal parts with a good Scotch whisky to make a Rusty Nail.

the essentials

Drambuie is a liqueur based on aged grain and malt whiskies and blended with heather honey syrup and a secret herbal essence that includes orange, cloves, vanilla, and cinnamon. It has a rich, malty, honeyed flavor, with a satisfyingly dry aftertaste of cinnamon and citrus tang. The only place in the world that produces it is the Drambuie Liqueur Company in Edinburgh. Any other liqueurs claiming to be Drambuie should only be used to remove limescale from kettles.

brands

Along with the classic fresh, malty flavor of Drambuie, try either of the following variations:

BLACK RIBBON

Containing a different infusion of herbs and spices, this variation of the original has a rich, peaty, fruit flavor with a biscuity aftertaste. Ideal for the Drambuie connoisseur looking to try something different.

DRAMBUIE CREAM

A perfect blend of Drambuie and cream, the bottle alone has won awards for being a design classic. And with such a delicious chocolatey-vanilla flavor, you'll forgive the slightly disconcerting aroma of Band-Aids upon first opening the bottle. A perfect late-night drink to round off a good meal or a night on the tiles.

sambuca

past and present

AN ITALIAN DRINK WITH A PERSONALITY TO MATCH, SAMBUCA IS A SMOOTH, SWEET, PASSIONATE LIQUEUR WITH A DISTINCTIVELY FIERY EDGE. GET HOOKED ON THIS FAMOUS LIQUEUR AND BEFORE YOU KNOW IT YOU'LL BE DONNING SHADES, RIDING VESPAS AROUND THE AMALFI COAST, GETTING INVOLVED IN FAMILY FEUDS, AND WAKING UP TO FIND A HORSE'S HEAD IN YOUR BED.

Sambuca was first produced in Civitavecchia—a town 50 miles from Rome—in the early 1800s by the Molinari family. Traditionally, it has always been served as an after-dinner drink: authentic Italian restaurants will even offer one "gratis," to help digest all those rich pasta dishes and pizza. But then those wily Italians with their sophisticated palates have always known a thing or two about good living. Why knock back handfuls of antacid tablets after a heavy meal when you can sip on a sweet, sensual liqueur instead?

The traditional way to drink sambuca is "con mosca," meaning "with flies," which does not require one to slurp it down with a handful of bluebottles, but actually involves floating three coffee beans on top of the liqueur and setting it alight. Legend decrees that for good luck it must be three, and only three, coffee beans in a glass of sambuca—any more or less and the god of misfortune will set your hair alight.

To perform the infamous "fire-breather," take a small mouthful of sambuca but don't swallow. After carefully wiping any stray droplets of the liqueur from your lips, tilt back your head and then—and this is where the phrase "choose your friends carefully" comes into play—have a friend light the sambuca in your mouth with a match. When you feel the drink burning, close your mouth and swallow. It certainly looks impressive, though if performed carelessly it could cost you a burned mouth or lips. And if you've got a beard, don't even go there.

Like all good drinks, sambuca has, at times, fallen prey to the fickle ways of fashion. During the golden period of Disco in the 1970s, a flaming sambuca was as essential to the Disco Diva as rollerblades, flares, and chest-hair. Nowadays it is more popular as a shot, owing to its high alcohol content and sweet flavor, and is often served neat or with ice. While puritans complain that setting light to a sambuca means burning away some of the precious alcohol, to drink it any other way is to miss out on all the fun.

CHRISTMAS PUDDING

- 1½ oz black sambuca
- 6 oz eggnog (best to raid your parents drinks' cabinet for this, rather than having to buy a bottle)

Mix the black sambuca and eggnog together and serve in an old-fashioned glass. It sounds revolting, but it tastes divine.

the essentials

- Sambuca is an anise liqueur, similar to arak, ouzo, and pastis in that it has a 40% alcohol content, is as clear as water, and has distinct flavors of mint and anise. Unlike those drinks, however, sambuca does not turn cloudy when water is added, has a much sweeter, smoother taste, and is by far the most popular of all the liquorice tasting cordials.
- In the world of sambuca there are two names: Molinari and Romana. These are the bastions of the anise liqueur, perfectly flavored and ubiquitous in every Italian-American's liquor cabinet.

brands

ROMANA BLACK SAMBUCA CLASSICA LIQUEUR

With the flavor of black liquorice and sweet anise, the first taste of this sambuca is like a really good spanking. Sure, the alcohol will burn your lips and tongue, but once you get past the burning sensation, it's very sweet, just like putting candy in your mouth. It also mixes well with coffee or espresso but, for goodness sake, don't add any more sugar.

ROMANA SAMBUCA CLASSICO

The winner of the Anglo Overseas Trophy for "Best Liqueur," Romana Sambuca Classico remains the world's leading brand of sambuca, and it has an inimitable sweet and smooth flavor that justifies the hype.

SAMBUCA DI AMORE CLASSICO LIQUEUR

For those with a really sweet tooth, this brand really pulls out the stops with its syrupy flavor and lingering sugary aftertaste. Excellent value for money, if you discount the inevitable dental bills from drinking too much of the stuff.

pimm's

past and present

A QUINTESSENTIALLY ENGLISH DRINK, PIMM'S WAS INVENTED NEARLY 200 YEARS AGO BY MR JAMES PIMM, THE OWNER OF A LONDON OYSTER BAR.

Oyster bars were, in their day, the closest equivalent Dickensian London had to fast food joints, and were places where gentlemen could wander in and consume a plate of oysters with a pint of stout or rum punch, before wandering home to preen their moustaches and read Oliver Twist. James, however, was a man of exceptional tastes, and wanted to serve something refreshing and sophisticated to his clients and Pimm's was entirely his own creation. This unique drink became extremely fashionable throughout much of London, and by the 1900s was being exported to the officers and gentlemen in the various British colonies around the world. Because of this, Pimm's has never really thrown off its rather snooty image, and has in fact rather wisely embraced it, remaining indelibly linked with images of English country lawns, rosy-cheeked girls playing croquet, and glorious summers days.

the essentials

Pimm's is a blend of gin, fruit extracts, liqueurs, and bitter herbs. The recipe remains a closely guarded secret and there are said to be only six people in the world who know it. Pimm's is available in two varieties: Number One, which is made with gin; and Number Six, made with vodka. Pimm's should be drunk by the pint, in a silver mug and—ideally—in the Oxford University Tennis Club, where it has been served free to members for the last 100 years.

HOW TO MAKE THE PERFECT PIMM'S

- Cut a cucumber into strips, slice an apple, orange, lemon, and lime.

- Fill a tall glass with ice.

- Add several drops of Angostura.

- Pour in one generous measure of Pimm's.

- Add a large measure of good quality gin.

- Top up the rest of the glass with three measures of lemonade or soda.

- Garnish with mint and the fruit and cucumber decorations.

- Find an old P. G. Wodehouse novel and a quiet corner of the bar.

campari

past and present

CAMPARI WAS INVENTED IN ITALY BY GASPARE CAMPARI, WHO—AFTER SETTING UP THE CAFFE CAMPARI COFFEESHOP IN MILAN IN 1862— LOCKED HIMSELF IN THE CELLARS, INTENT ON CREATING A BRAND NEW BEVERAGE. AFTER FIVE YEARS OF DABBLING, EXPERIMENTING, AND A MILD FLIRTATION WITH DEVIL WORSHIP, HE HIT UPON A UNIQUE AND BITTER, TANGY, RED LIQUEUR. BEING A HOT-BLOODED AND PROUD ITALIAN, CAMPARI NATURALLY NAMED THIS NEW DRINK AFTER HIMSELF. IT WAS AN INSTANT HIT WITH THE SOPHISTICATED CLIENTELE OF MILAN AND, WITH THE BIRTH OF THE COCKTAIL ERA, WENT ON TO BE A BEST-SELLING DRINK WORLDWIDE.

A victim of its own success, however, in recent years Campari's association with bourgeois cocktail parties has done much to damage its image. While bitter spirits remain popular in Italy, Campari—like vermouth and the other lesser-known cocktail cupboard stalwarts—still suffers from serious under-appreciation.

As with so many things of refinement (such as caviar, truffles, or peanut butter), Campari is usually regarded as being an acquired taste. According to its inventor, Gaspare, "It is necessary to drink Campari three times before you enjoy it."

In an age where gratuitous amounts of sugar are added to nearly everything we eat or drink, the bitter taste of Campari can seem... well, too bitter. However, for those willing to see beyond the fickleness of fashion and sugar addiction, Campari is waiting to be rediscovered. It is an excellent aperitif, a truly distinctive drink, and— for the uninitiated—a bold journey into pastures new.

the essentials

- Campari is a bittersweet, ruby-red liquor, the result of a unique blend of 68 herbs, spices, peels, and bitters, mellowed in selected spirit.
- As an aperitif, Campari should be served in a frozen glass with no ice.
- When serving with a mixer, always blend an equal amount of the mixer with Campari, to optimize the release of its bittersweet flavors.
- The classic Campari mixer is, of course, soda, although it works equally well with tonic water, orange juice, or grapefruit juice.
- When adding a garnish to a drink containing Campari, always use a slice of orange: lemon can impair the real flavor.
- In 1932, the company released "Campari and Soda," the first in a flood of pre-mixed cocktails and one of the few of its kind to have lasted the distance. It was, in many ways, the great granddaddy of the Alcopop.

WINE

past and present

BEING A NATURAL PROCESS THAT OCCURS WITHOUT HUMAN INTERFERENCE, WINE ACTUALLY PRE-DATES CIVILIZATION. THE "NECTAR OF THE GODS" MAY HAVE FIRST BEEN DISCOVERED BY ACCIDENT BY SOME UNWITTING CAVEMAN, WHO—FINDING THE TASTE AND EFFECTS TO HIS LIKING—WOULD HAVE STAGGERED HOME TO TELL THE TRIBE ABOUT HIS DISCOVERY (THOUGH NOT BEFORE SINGING A FEW BAWDY SONGS ABOUT DINOSAURS AND FALLING OVER A LOT).

While the inebriated caveman may just be the product of my imagination, tomb paintings of pharaohs engaged in the art of wine-making suggest that as early as 4000 BC the wily Egyptians had already figured out that an ox kebab goes down well with a good bottle of red. In fact, they had even discovered the advantages of putting a cork in a bottle and—more importantly—worked out how to get it out again. Wine is also celebrated in the writings of Homer (the Greek poet, not Bart's dad), was said in the Bible to have been cultivated by Noah, and is known to have been used by early Minoan, Greek, and Etruscan civilizations.

With the rise of the Roman Empire and, later, Christianity, by the third century AD the first vineyards of Bordeaux and Burgundy had sprung up, as monastic communities developed methods of vineyard tending and cellarwork, which later spread to Spain and Germany. By the 1200s, vineyards were flourishing throughout much of Europe. Around this time a French monastic group, the Cistercians, developed the idea of creating a homogenous plot of land in a particular area, dedicated to an individual flavor and style of wine. The Cistercians were not a bunch who did things by halves—they even tasted the soil in different regions to assess quality for wine-growing. While their dedication and grueling labors meant that most Cistercians died by their late twenties (either of sheer exhaustion or from being sick of the sight of grapes), their method spread throughout Europe, leading the way for the method of wine type recognition we know today—through the grape and area of origin.

In the US, the first venture into winemaking began in 1769 with the arrival of a Franciscan Monk, Junipero Cerro, who founded a Catholic Mission in San Diego and began producing wine. These days the US—like Australia, New Zeland, and South Africa—can hold its own with the best wine producers in the world.

red wine

the essentials

- Red wine is made from fermented grape juice. Yeast extracts, existing naturally on grape surfaces, come into contact with sugar in the grape juice and turn it into alcohol.
- Wine is ultimately derived from the carbon dioxide in the air, which penetrates the leaves of the vine and is converted, by photosynthesis, into starches.
- In red-wine production the skins, seeds, and juice are all fermented together.
- Wine is usually aged in wooden containers made of oak or redwood, which also contribute to the flavor. The wood-aging process may last many months or several years, depending on the wine and the quality desired.
- Some wines are aged in bottles before being sold. Red wines especially may profit from 2 to 20 years of bottle aging, though in most cases it's best to just drink 'em quick.
- Red wine takes its color, not from the juice, as most people presume, but from the skin, which provides tannin, an important factor in the way wine tastes.
- One species of grape, *Vitis vinifera*, is used for nearly all the wine made in the world. From this species as many as 4,000 varieties of grape have been developed.
- While the benefits of red wine have long been the subject of folklore, recent scientific research has shown that a couple of glasses per day are good for the heart: red wine interferes with the production of a body chemical that is vital to the process that clogs up arteries and increases the risk of a heart attack. It may also help kill off breast cancer cells. Having several glasses before your croissant and coffee in the morning, as the French are prone to do, however, pushes the theory to extremes and is probably not a good idea.

Despite what wine snobs may tell you, screw lids on wine bottles are, in fact, more practical and economical than corks and do not decrease the quality of the wine. They may, however, one day call an end to the lovely corkscrew ritual of:

- Squeezing a bottle of wine between both thighs.

- Grunting and going red faced as you yank on the corkscrew with all your might.

- Swearing a lot.

- Ending up with red wine all down your pants.

red wine styles

SYRAH (OR SHIRAZ)

A hearty red wine that goes very well with rich, red meat dishes. Grown in France's Rhone Valley, California, Washington State, and Australia, Syrah has a black-fruit aroma and spicy tang. While this grape can be used to produce some of the world's finest rich red wines, it can also make some of the blandest. With Syrah it's always worth spending that extra bit more to guarantee good quality.

MERLOT

A superb blending grape, the "darling of the California wine industry," and a good introduction for those relatively new to the complex world of red wine, Merlot goes well with most meals (with the possible exception of liver and ice-cream) and is best produced in Bordeaux and the US (particularly the West Coast, Long Island, and Washington State's Columbia region). If price is an issue, Bulgaria, Hungary, and Romania offer some decent Merlots at a very modest price.

CABERNET SAUVIGNON

Produced in France, California, Chile, and Australia, Cabernet Sauvignon is widely accepted as one of the world's best varieties of red wine. Full-bodied, firm, and fruity, this wine goes well with prepared red meat. If you want the best, go for Bordeaux every time, but be prepared to pay through the nose; with few exceptions, the cheap to mid-price Cabernet's are dreadful. Of the Californian varieties, those grown in the Stags Leap District and hillside sites of Nappa and Sonoma remain the best.

PINOT NOIR

A noble, fruity fellow, yet hard to please (the grape is notoriously difficult to grow). When it's right, it surpasses all competition; when it's wrong, it's very wrong and can taste like supermarket jam. The best stuff is from Burgundy, Romania, the upper Loire valley, California (notably Santa Barbara), Oregon, and New Zealand. Buy it from anywhere else and you could be asking for trouble. Ideal with grilled salmon, chicken, and lamb.

SANGIOVESE

Wine is often called the nectar of the gods, but this is the only grape named after a god (Sangiovese means "blood of Jove"). Italian Chianti, probably the best-known wine in the world, comes from Sangiovese grapes. Of course that doesn't mean it's the best wine—far from it. In the past, most cheap Chiantis had a thin, acidic, abrasive flavor, but recent changes in the Tuscan wine industry and experiments in blending have given these traditionally cheap wines a new lease of life. Try a moderately-priced Chianti with spaghetti bolognese, pizza, or a rich pasta dish and you may be pleasantly surprised.

ZINFANDEL

Unique to California, this zesty, versatile grape with a strong berry flavor is used to make rich, heavy red wines that pair excellently with tomato-sauce pastas, pizza, and grilled and barbecued meats. Zinfandel is also used to make (very bad) white and blushed wine, so make sure to specify red when ordering!

white wine

SEEN SOMEWHAT AS ROBIN IS TO
BATMAN, WHITE WINE IS OFTEN UNFAIRLY
DISMISSED AS THE WEEDY COUSIN OF
RED AND RARELY GIVEN THE ATTENTION IT
DESERVES. BUT WHILE ROBIN REMAINS AN
IRRITATING APPENDAGE, TO IGNORE WHITE
WINE IS TO MISS OUT ON A FASCINATING RANGE
OF FLAVORS AND A DRINK THAT ACCOMPANIES
AND ENHANCES A WIDE RANGE OF FOODS.

the essentials

- White wine is produced in a similar way to red with the exception that, for fermentation, all skins and stems are removed to avoid any color being added.
- White wine is normally aged for less time than red—some might age for up to a year to give the correct amount of flavor, while others can be bottled immediately.
- White wine should be served chilled, though not too cold—half an hour in the refrigerator should be the optimum time.
- White wines are normally drinkable upon purchase of the bottle, though some do benefit from a few years of aging.

white wine styles

CHARDONNAY

The world's most popular grape, Chardonnay is unfussy about climate and grows equally well in the cold, gray climate of northern France (where it is used to make Burgundy) and in the hot vineyards of Australia. In recent years, it has really hit its prime growing in California, where a wide range of excellent varieties are on offer. Chardonnay is usually dry and goes best with poultry, seafood, and cheeses such as gruyère, provolone, and brie. It is relatively inexpensive—a surprisingly good Chardonnay can cost under $10, though there is so much on the market it can be a little overwhelming knowing where to start. If it's cheap but reliable you're after, go for Chilean; if you've got money to spend, the pricier Californians are usually excellent. For the very best, white burgundy is top of the range (don't look for Chardonnay on the label—you won't find it) in flavor and price, so make sure someone else is paying.

RIESLING (PRONOUNCED REEEEEZLING!)

Simply the best grape in the world, Riesling can offer a full range of flavors from dry to sweet, light to fruity, and oily to waxy. It's the perfect white wine to be drunk on its own (though its sophisticated flavor goes very well with oriental dishes, seafood, and even chocolate). For those who don't like their wines too sweet, the Californian varieties are best avoided in favor of those grown in the Rhine Valley in Germany or Alsace in France—these tend to be more aromatic and have a more balanced flavor. Being a difficult grape to grow, Riesling can be expensive, and to truly appreciate a good Riesling takes time, but it is time (and money) well spent.

SAUVIGNON BLANC (PRONOUNCED SO-VEEN-YAWN BLAH)

A good, versatile light white wine, ranging from dry to sweet and with dominating flavors ranging from sour green fruits of apples, pears, and gooseberries through to tropical fruits of melon, mango, and blackcurrant.

Sauvignon blanc is widely grown throughout the world, though the best varieties remain those produced in New Zealand, and in Bordeaux and the Upper Loire Valley in France. Australia's Sauvignon Blancs should be treated with caution: they can be a bit hit and miss, with many varieties flat and lacking the fruit flavor. In the US it is sometimes called "Fumé Blanc."

WHITE ZINFANDEL

Although a hugely popular wine in the US (one out of every 10 bottles of table wine opened in the US is White Zinfandel), this wine, as a Monty Python character once said, "should only be used for hand-to-hand combat." Often cheap, sour, and lacking in complexity and richness, it's best kept for cooking or to get dried egg out of a pan. If I were feeling a little kinder, I could say it is young, sweet, easy on the palate, and delicious with pasta dishes, fish, pork, and other "lighter" meals. But I'm not.

CHENIN BLANC

Sweet, rich, and with an intense, fascinating aroma, Chenin is an all-round excellent wine. It is produced in many places around the world, including California, Chile, Australia, New Zealand, and, most notably, South Africa. However, many of these wines (particularly those from hotter growing areas, which produce grapes that are much more neutral and much less flavorsome) don't compare to the quality of the top French efforts. For the best, go for those grown in the Loire Valley of France. For the worst, try the Australian, which smells and tastes of wet dogs.

" IF WHITE WINE GOES WITH FISH,

DO WHITE GRAPES GO WITH SUSHI? "

COMEDIAN EDDIE IZZARD

champagne

past and present

THE CHOICE OF THE RICH AND FAMOUS, A SYMBOL OF OPULENCE AND DECADENCE, AN EBULLIENT WINE WITH A BIG PERSONALITY, CHAMPAGNE HAS NEVER LOST ITS FOOTING AS THE KING OF DRINKS, UBIQUITOUS AT EVERY CELEBRATORY RITUAL, FROM TOASTING THE BRIDE AND GROOM TO LAUNCHING A SHIP. AND, LIKE ALL GOOD INVENTIONS, IT CAME ABOUT BY ACCIDENT.

A region of France long before it was a sparkling wine, Champagne held a reputation for producing excellent vino as far back as the Roman times. Traditionally, it had always produced "still" red wine, but with growing competition (and petty rivalry) from the vineyards of Burgundy, Champagne's wine producers began to experiment and branch out by blending different grapes to create new forms of light-colored wines. While these proved to be a success, it was then that something rather unexpected occurred.

Owing to Champagne's cold climates and short growing seasons, the grapes in the area had to be picked late in the year, and with the ensuing winter months curtailing the fermentation process, there was rarely enough time for the yeasts to convert all the sugar in the pressed grape juice into alcohol. The following spring, as the bottles were shipped abroad, the fermentation process would start up again, but this time inside the bottles, creating carbon dioxide that remained trapped within. To the surprise of its recipients, this wine arrived packed with bubbles, attracting a lot of attention in both England and France. It wasn't long before this new "sparkling" wine was the height of fashion amongst the higher echelons of society.

Unfortunately for the producers of this new wine, the unpredictable nature of the second fermentation meant that wandering the cellars in springtime was much akin to standing under a coconut tree in the height of summer—up to 40% of the produce was being lost from exploding bottles. Until along came Dom Pérignon, a Benedictine Monk at the abbey at Hautvillers, who wisely saw that using stronger glass for the bottles and sealing them with Spanish corks (instead of wood and hemp stoppers) could drastically reduce their cleaning bills. A springtime visit to the cellar still remained a dangerous game of Russian roulette, however, until 1836, when a pharmacist, Monsieur François (yes, that really was his name), invented the sucre-oenometre, which measured the amount of sugar needed to stimulate the second fermentation in the bottles, thus stabilizing the buildup of gas.

With the growing success of Champagne over the next two centuries, producers of sparkling wine in nearby regions started to cash in on the name. The Champagne producers naturally took umbrage to this, and—as the French are prone to do—downed tools and rioted. Their demands for exclusive rights to the name were eventually met, and since 1927 the name Champagne has remained heavily protected. Nowadays, its producers have a whole team of venomous, psychotic lawyers dedicated to protecting the name.

Although a huge slump in sales followed World War I, the Bolshevik Revolution (no more orders from Imperial Russia), Prohibition, and the Great Depression, sales of Champagne have continued to grow since the 1940s. De rigueur for weddings, parties, and decadent breakfasts, and for throwing at large sea-faring vessels, Champagne remains ever-fashionable and, as a mark of its status as the celebratory drink of choice, more Champagne is drunk today by more people than ever before.

the essentials

- There are essentially three types of Champagne: Blanc de Blancs, produced from white grapes (usually Chardonnay); Blanc de Noirs, produced from black grapes; and Rosé, where a little red wine is added to the mix.
- The sweetness of Champagne is dependent entirely on the amount of sugar present in the dosage, ranging through Brut (the driest), Extra Dry (dry but, confusingly, not as dry as Brut!), and Demi-sec (the sweetest).
- There are around 250 million bubbles in every bottle of Champagne (though I've no idea who counted them).
- The classic saucer-shaped Champagne glass is said to have been modeled on the breasts of Marie-Antoinette.
- Despite what you may have read elsewhere, dangling the handle of a silver spoon in the neck of a Champagne bottle makes absolutely no difference in sustaining the bubbles in the bottle. If you want to stop Champagne going flat, the best solution is to drink it.
- The smaller the bubbles, the better the quality of the Champagne.

what to buy

- The label on a good bottle of Champagne should display the quality of grapes used. Ratings of "Grand Cru" or "Premier Cru" are the best.
- For the classic Champagne taste, always go for Brut.
- Undisputed premium brands and styles include Krug, Moët & Chandon's Dom Pérignon, Pol Roger's Sir Winston Churchill, La Grande Dame, Ayala, Canard-Duchêne, Reims, Laurent Perrier, Pinot Noir, Brut Rosé, and Epernay.
- The years 1988, 1989, and 1990 were all exceptional for Champagne: pick a vintage from these years and you can't go too far wrong.
- If you're a fan of 007, the obvious choice would be Bollinger. This Champagne of reassuringly good quality has featured over seven times in the Bond films alone—and you can rest assured that Mr Bond is a man of exquisite taste.
- For those on a budget, California and Australia have, of late, being producing some viable alternatives that taste as good as the real thing. Roederer, Taittinger Domaine Carneros, Greg Norman, and Westport Rivers are all excellent quality dry Champagnes that won't break the bank. And Cava from Spain isn't bad either.

HOW TO SERVE CHAMPAGNE

It's all very well being able to afford a good bottle of champers, but shaking the stuff up, letting the cork ricochet around the room eight times and then spilling most of it on the floor is a technique best left to racing drivers and hosts of frat parties. Adherence to the saying "the ear's gain is the palate's loss" is, of course, the correct policy. The art of serving Champagne lies in the gentleness with which the cork is removed, and the delicacy of the pouring.

When opening an uncorked bottle, place the fingers over the cork and gently turn the bottle (not the cork), taking care to keep the bottle angled about 45% away from the body (and anyone who might be in firing range). Rather than giving off a loud pop, the cork should merely sigh—as if having had its neck stroked by Michelle Pfeiffer—to minimize the loss of those valuable bubbles.

After the neck of the bottle has been wiped with a clean piece of linen, pour the Champagne into glasses about one inch at a time, to allow the froth to settle each time. It should usually take three servings if using proper Champagne glasses, and about 100 if using a pint glass.

Champagne should be served chilled at around 45°F (7°C). This is best achieved by placing the bottle in a bucket of half ice/half water for 30 minutes, or in a refrigerator for 3-4 hours.

bar code

IN THE US ONE WOULD SAY
"I'll have a beer, please."

FINNISH
"Olut mulle, kiitos."
(O-loot moolek kee-tos)

CHINESE
"请给我一杯啤酒"
(Ching gay woh ee bay pee joh)

FRENCH
"Une bière, s'il vous plaît."
(Oon bee-air, seel voo pleh)

CZECH/SLOVAK
"Pivo, prosím."
(Pee-vo, pro-seem)

GERMAN
"Ein Bier, bitte."
(Ine beer, bitt-uh)

DANISH
"Jeg vil gerne have en øl."
(Yay vil geh-neh heh en url)

GREEK
"Μια μπυρα παρακαλω"
(Mee-a beer-a paraka-loh)

DUTCH
"Een bier, alsjeblieft."
(Un beer, ahls-yer-bleeft)

HUNGARIAN
"Egy pohár sört kérek."
(Edj pohar shurt kayrek)

ESPERANTO
"Unu bieron, mi petas."
(Oo-noo bee-airon, mee peh-tahs)

ICELANDIC
"Einn bjór, takk."
(Ay-dn byohr tahk)

ENGLISH
"A pint of your best, my good man."

IRISH
"Beoir amháin, le do thoil."
(Byohr awoyn, lyeh doh hull)

SCOTS GAELIC
"Leann, mas e do thoil e."
(Lyawn mahs eh doh hawl eh)

ITALIAN
"Una birra, per favore."
(Oo-na beer-ra, pair fa-vo-re)

SPANISH (LAT. AM.)
"Una cerveza, por favor."
(Oo-na ser-veh-sa, por fa-vor)

JAPANESE
"ビール(を)一本下さい。"
(Bee-ru ip-pon ku-da-sai)

SPANISH (SPAIN)
"Una cerveza, por favor."
(Oo-na thair-veh-tha, por fa-vor)

NORWEGIAN
"En øl, takk."
(Ehn url tahk)

SWEDISH
"En öl, tack."
(Ehn irl, tahk)

POLISH
"Jedno piwo, prosze."
(Yed-no peevo prosha)

WELSH
"Cwrw os gwelwch in dda."
(Koo-roh ohs gwel-ookh-un-thah)

PORTUGUESE
"Uma cerveja, por favor."
(Oo-ma ser-vay-ja, poor fa-vohr)

YIDDISH
"א ביר, זייט אזוי גוט"
(A beer, zeit a-zoy goot)

RUSSIAN
"пиво, пожалуйста"
(Ahd-na pee-vah pah-zha-loosta)

how to be a cocktail
connoisseur

essential equipment

- Spirits and mixers (soft drinks)

- Condiments (bitters, cream, salt, Tabasco, etc.)

- Garnishes (slice of orange, lemon, lime, cucumber, olives, dead flies, etc.)

- Cocktail shaker and Boston shaker

- Ice

- Ice bucket and lid

- Ice tongs

- Ice crusher (using a rolling pin and plastic bag can get messy!)

- Strainer

- Dishcloth

- Juice squeezer

- Bottle opener

- Corkscrew

- Jigger (measure)

- Assorted glasses (Martini glass, old-fashioned, highball, marguerita, shot glass, Collins, champagne flute)

- Bar spoon (for making cocktails with several layers)

- Smoking jacket

- Cigarette holder

- Vinyl only copies of albums by Nelson Riddle, Xavier Cuget, Esquivel, Martin Denny, Frank Sinatra, Sammy Davis Junior, and Dean Martin.

THE ART OF USING A COCKTAIL SHAKER

Use a cocktail shaker that is bigger than the amount of liquid required; you'll need plenty of room for the liquid and ice to move around inside.

Don't be shy—shake vigorously.

Shake your cocktail until the outside starts to get very cold. The optimum shaking time is 10 seconds. If frostbite begins to kick in, you've been doing it too long.

Never put your tongue on a cold cocktail shaker.

Refrain from juggling the bottles and shaker, despite what you may have seen in Tom Cruise films—it is dangerous and unforgivably tacky.

Wrap the shaker in a dishcloth— it will protect your hands from the cold and insulate your shaker from your own body heat.

Take your glasses from the freezer, crank up Frank, and you're all ready to serve a killer cocktail!

tips for tips

THE WORD TIP ORIGINATES FROM THE ACRONYM T.I.P. (TO INSURE PROMPTNESS).

Many people, particularly in Europe, consider tipping to be merely an act of goodwill, but in certain parts of the world, the people serving your drinks may well rely on tips to ensure a reasonable wage at the end of the day. Memorize the coins below and you need never worry again about whether leaving a handful of cents at the end of the night will delight, confuse, or insult the poor guy who has spent the last four hours lighting cigarettes, pouring you double brandies, and listening to your relentless drunken rhetoric...

AUSTRALIA
Not necessary.

CHINA
Not necessary.

FRANCE
Leave some small change or just round up the bill.

BELGIUM
Leave some small change or just round up the bill.

GREECE
Leave some small change or just round up the bill.

GERMANY
Not necessary.

CANADA
Tipping in Canadian bars ranges from 10-20%, depending on whether the city is French or English Canadian.

HOLLAND
Tipping is welcomed but not expected.

ITALY
Leave some small change or just round up the bill.

SCANDINAVIA
Not necessary.

SWITZERLAND
Leave some small change or just round up the bill.

SPAIN
5% in bars and cafés for the waiter.

JAPAN
Not necessary.

UNITED KINGDOM
Not necessary, though if you're impressed with a barman/barwoman's service (or you wish to flirt/chat with them), you can offer to buy them a drink. As they aren't allowed to drink when serving, they will usually keep the cash as a tip, with the promise to "have one (a drink) later."

MEXICO
Tipping is expected and generosity is appreciated.

NEW ZEALAND
Not necessary.

UNITED STATES
The etiquette here is usually to put a dollar or two into a pot at the bar. Since you usually pay at the end, this doesn't get too expensive and means that on your next visit you should expect more generous quantities if served by the same bar staff.

pickups & put-downs

pickups

Let's be honest—people don't just go to bars to drink. As well as playing games, socializing, and confessing all their terrible crimes and misdemeanors with the barstaff, men and women frequently visit bars to flirt with each other. And a bar is an ideal place for this; alcohol is the ideal social drug for washing away inhibitions, loosening the tongue, and stimulating the libido. As a consequence men (and, to a lesser extent, women), needing something to say when starting a conversation, often resort to chat-up lines. From the timeless, "What's a nice girl like you doing in a place like this?" to such saccharine-coated efforts as "Are you lost? 'cos heaven's a long way from here," chat-up lines are the last bastion of the desperate and unimaginative, but they remain strangely enduring. Below is a wide selection for you to do with as you please, presented on a sliding scale of vulgarity...

- Did the sun come out, or did you just smile at me?
- Didn't I see you on the cover of *Vogue*?
- I think I can die happy now, because I've just seen a piece of heaven.
- If you were a bogey I'd pick you first.
- What's that on your face? Looks like beauty. Let me rub it off… Hey! it's not coming off!
- What's your first name? Hmm, that goes well with my last name.
- If I could rearrange the alphabet, I'd put U and I together.
- The only thing your eyes haven't told me is your name.
- Do you believe in love at first sight, or should I walk by again?
- I'm fighting the urge to make you the happiest woman on Earth tonight.
- Pardon me, I seem to have lost my phone number. Could I borrow yours?
- Baby, I'm no Fred Flintstone, but I can make your Bedrock!
- Be unique and different—say "Yes."
- If this bar is a meat market, you must be the prime rib.
- Do those legs go all the way up?
- I think I could fall madly in bed with you.
- I wonder what our children will look like.
- I'll cook you dinner if you cook me breakfast.
- Your legs must be tired, because you've been running through my mind all night.
- That dress/shirt looks great on you—it'd look better on my bedroom floor.

- Got any Irish/Scottish/Welsh/Indian, etc. in you? (Answer: "No.") You want some?
- Do you know the difference between a sandwich and a blow job? No? Do you want to have lunch?
- Do you know what winks and fucks like a tiger? (Then you wink.)

- I'd like to give you a massage—from the inside.
- I heard your ankles were having a party… want to invite your knickers down?
- I've had quite a bit to drink, and you're beginning to look pretty good.
- I like your ass—can I wear it as a hat?
- Gee, that's a nice set of legs. What time do they open?

put-downs

Of course, being armed with a series of tacky chat-up lines isn't half as important as knowing how to get rid of someone when you're on the receiving end. If you do find yourself in that uncomfortable situation (and I'm talking mainly to the ladies here now), flex that ironic eyebrow muscle, get the right acerbic tone in your voice, and try out a few of these for size:

- I've seen you somewhere before. That's why I don't go there any more.
- Yes, that seat is empty, and this one will be too, if you sit down.
- I'm just sitting here waiting for some idiot to come along and bore me with pathetic pickup lines.
- Your place or mine? How about both? You go to your place, and I'll go to mine.
- What's my sign? No Entry.
- I like my eggs unfertilized in the morning.
- Would I like to go back to your place? Well, I don't know. Will two people fit under a rock?
- You're here to fulfil my every sexual fantasy? You mean you can lend me a donkey and a great dane?

- Could you ask me out from a distance? Your breath is bleaching my eyebrows.
- Sure, if you saw me naked you'd die happy. But if I saw you naked I'd die laughing.
- If you know how to please a woman/man, then please leave me alone.
- You want to give yourself to me? Sorry, I don't accept cheap, nasty gifts.
- Do you know what I want from you? I want you to go away.
- Sorry, I don't date outside my species.
- I'll see you in my dreams—if I eat too much cheese.
- I need a real man. Do you know where I can find one?
- Ask you out? Okay, get out.

"a man walks into a bar.."

A man walks into a bar holding an alligator. He asks the bartender, "Do you serve lawyers here?" The bartender says, "Sure we do!"

"Good" replied the man. "Give me a beer, and I'll have a lawyer for my alligator."

A man walks into a bar and sits down next to a lady and a dog. The man asks, "Does your dog bite?"

The lady answers, "Never!" The man reaches out to pet the dog and the dog bites him. He says, "I thought you said your dog doesn't bite!"

The woman replies, "He doesn't. But this isn't my dog."

A man walks into a bar. Two North Dakotans are there, buying drinks for everyone in the place, slapping them on the back, and whooping it up. "What's the occasion?" says the man. "We just finished a jigsaw puzzle, and it only took us two months!" say the two guys. The man replies, "Two months! What's the big deal? Jigsaw puzzle shouldn't take two months!"

"Oh yeah?" say the two men, "On the box it said two to three years."

A man walks into a bar with a slab of asphalt under his arm and says,

"A beer please, and one for the road."

A penguin walks into a bar, goes to the counter, and asks the bartender, "Have you seen my brother?"

The bartender says, "I don't know, what does he look like?"

A man walks into a bar and sees a dog sitting in a chair playing poker with a couple of guys. The man says to the barman, "Is that dog really playing poker?" The barman says, "He is, but he's not very good."

"Why's that?" asks the man.

"Every time he gets a good hand he wags his tail."

A man walks into a bar and says, "Get me a drink before the trouble starts." The barman pours him a drink. He swallows it down and says, "Get me another drink before the trouble starts." The barman gives him another drink. The man sinks that one as fast as the first and says again, "Get me a drink before the trouble starts." So the barman says, "When exactly is this trouble going to start?" The man says, "As soon as you realize that I don't have any money."

A man walks into a bar, sits down and hears a small voice say, "You look nice today."

A few minutes later he again hears a small voice, "That's a nice shirt."

The guy asks the bartender, "What is that?"

The bartender says, "Those are the peanuts. They're complimentary!"

A man walks into a bar and there is a horse behind the bar serving drinks. The guy is just staring at the horse when the horse says, "What are you staring at? Haven't you ever seen a horse serving drinks before?"

The guy says, "No it's not that, I just never thought the unicorn would sell the place."

A horse walks into a bar and the bartender asks "Why the long face?"

A woman goes into a bar and asks for a double entendre. So the bartender gave her one.

A neutron walks into a bar and orders a beer. The bartender sets the beer down and says, "For you, no charge!"

A kangaroo walks into a bar. He orders a beer. The bartender says, "That'll be $10. You know, we don't get many kangaroos coming in here, you know."

The kangaroo says, "At $10 a beer, it's not hard to understand."

A dog with his leg wrapped in bandages hobbles into a saloon. He sidles up to the bar and announces: "I'm lookin' fer the man that shot my paw."

A grasshopper hops into a bar. The bartender says, "You're quite a celebrity around here. We've even got a drink named after you."

The grasshopper says, "You've got a drink named Steve?"

A skeleton walks into a bar and says, "Gimme a beer, and a mop."

A polar bear, a giraffe, and a penguin walk into a bar. The bartender says, "What is this? Some kind of joke?"

A man walks into a bar. Ouch!

no-nos and go-gos

COUNTRY	MINIMUM DRINKING AGE IN BARS	MINIMUM PURCHASING AGE
Australia	18	18
Belgium	15	16
Canada	In Alberta, Manitoba, and Quebec, it is 18; in all other provinces, 19	In Alberta, Manitoba, and Quebec, it is 18; in all other provinces, 19
Czech Republic	18	18
Denmark	18	15
England	18	18
Finland	18	18
France	16	16
Germany	16 (beer and wine) 18 (spirits)	16 (beer and wine) 18 (spirits)
Greece	18	18
Hong Kong	18	18
Ireland	18	18
Israel	18	18
Italy	16	16
Japan	20	20
Mexico	18	-
Netherlands	18	18
New Zealand	18	18
Norway	18 (beer and wine) 20 (spirits)	18 (beer and wine) 20 (spirits)
Portugal	18	18
Russia	21	18
South Africa	18	18
Spain	16	16
United States	21	21

tricks & treats

bar tricks

THE FOLLOWING BAR TRICKS ARE DESIGNED TO BE PERFORMED WITH ON-HAND ITEMS FOUND AROUND ANY BAR: BOTTLES, GLASSES, MONEY, PEOPLE, MATCHES, CIGARS, NAPKINS, ETC. THEY CAN BE USED TO ENTERTAIN, AMUSE, INFURIATE, ASTOUND, IRRITATE, AND—MOST IMPORTANTLY—TO EARN YOURSELF A FREE DRINK.

THREE IN ONE

YOU WILL NEED:
• four shots

THE CHALLENGE:
that you can finish three shots before your participant finishes their one shot.

METHOD:

1 Establish the rule that your challenger can't start their shot until you start your second glass, with the added proviso that they can never touch or disturb any of your glasses.

2 Drink your first glass and place it over the top of their shot glass... upside down!

3 Casually finish your other two glasses, while they sit there helpless.

THE LEVITATING OLIVE

YOU WILL NEED:
• an olive
• a brandy snifter

THE CHALLENGE:
that you can place the olive inside the brandy snifter without touching it yourself, scooping it up with the snifter, or rolling it off the bar into the snifter.

METHOD:

1 With the olive on the bar, place the brandy snifter over the olive.

2 Slowly slide the brandy snifter in a circle around the olive.

3 As the olive rolls around the inside walls of the snifter, centrifugal force will hold it in place.

4 Once the olive is spinning around the middle of the snifter, flip the snifter upright and place it on the bar.

! TIP IT IS WORTH PRACTICING THIS BEFORE PLACING ANY BETS—THE OLIVE HAS A TENDENCY TO COME OUT OF THE SNIFTER AS YOU FLIP IT UPRIGHT.

 THREE COIN CON

YOU WILL NEED:
• three quarters

THE CHALLENGE:
to get a free drink.

METHOD:

1 Place three quarters on the bar, heads up.

2 Ask your victim, "What do you see?", to which the usual reply should be, "Three heads!" or "Three quarters."

3 Say, "I see two quarters. If I'm wrong, will you promise to buy me a drink?"

4 After pressuring your victim to agree, simply say "I am wrong. Can I now have my free drink?"

1 + 1 + 1 = ?

! **TIP** KEEP A POKER FACE WHEN MAKING THE BET. IT'S A GOOD IDEA TO HAVE WITNESSES TO YOUR VICTIM'S PROMISE, IN CASE HE TRIES TO BACK OUT OF THIS LUDICROUS CONTRACT.

THE 50-CENT COCKTAIL

YOU WILL NEED:
- an expensive cocktail, bought by your victim
- a cocktail napkin

THE CHALLENGE:
to get an expensive cocktail bought for you for just 50 cents.

METHOD:

1 Cover the victim's drink with a cocktail napkin.

2 Say, "I bet you 50 cents that without touching the glass, napkin, or any straws, I can drink that entire cocktail."

3 Bring up the point about possibly putting a straw through the napkin and say again, "I won't touch anything!"

4 Once your victim has conceded, slowly take off the napkin and enjoy the drink.

5 Push the 50 cents to your victim. Their expensive cocktail just cost you 50 cents!

! WARNING IT'S PROBABLY BEST TO ONLY TRY THIS TRICK ON FRIENDS OR COMPANIONS WHO CAN SEE THE FUNNY SIDE; YOU DON'T WANT TO END UP WITH A BLACK EYE, OR WORSE!

CLEVER SALT AND PEPPER

YOU WILL NEED:
- a salt packet
- a pepper packet
- a small plastic comb

THE CHALLENGE:
to separate a mixed pile of salt and pepper.

METHOD:

1 Make a small mound of salt on the bar, about the size of a quarter.

2 Sprinkle a small amount of pepper on top of the salt.

3 Bet your victim that you can get the pepper off the salt without disturbing it.

4 Once they have conceded, take your plastic comb and comb your hair a few times.

5 As you hold the comb over the salt and pepper, the static electricity will suck the pepper off the salt (provided that humidity levels in the bar are low!).

FLAMING SUGAR

YOU WILL NEED:
• two sugar cubes
• a lighter
• an ashtray

THE CHALLENGE:
to set a sugar cube alight.

METHOD:

1 Hand someone a sugar cube and a lighter.

2 Challenge them to set the cube aflame using the lighter.

3 The cube may smoke and smolder but, try as they may, it will not catch on fire.

4 Once they have given up, rub your sugar cube in the ash of an ashtray.

5 Now hold a flame to the sugar cube—it should light up right away.

WARNING MAKE SURE YOU HAVE AN ASHTRAY ON HAND WHEN DOING THIS TRICK, AS YOU WILL WANT TO DROP THE SUGAR CUBE IN IT PRETTY SHARPISH ONCE IT HAS BEEN SET ALIGHT.

HAIR OF THE ICE

YOU WILL NEED:
- two ice cubes
- some salt
- two pieces of human hair

THE CHALLENGE:
to pick up an ice cube with a human hair.

METHOD:

1 Let your participant try the trick. While they may try twisting or tying it around the ice cube, they will not, however, be able to get the ice cube off the bar.

2 When they have given up, place the ice cube on the bar, take your strand of human hair and place it across the top of the ice cube.

3 Take a little salt and sprinkle it on top of the hair and ice cube.

4 The salt will cause the ice cube to re-freeze around the hair and in just a few seconds you will be able to gently lift the cube off of the bar.

PHONE-OMENAL!

YOU WILL NEED:
- two cell phones
- a piece of paper
- a pen
- one stooge
- one victim

THE CHALLENGE:
to demonstrate the ancient art of remote sensing.

METHOD:

1 Get your stooge to leave the bar with their cell phone at the ready.

2 Once they are out of sight, get your victim to write down a playing card on a piece of paper and show you.

3 Phone your friend.

4 When you get through to them, say nothing, pretending that they have yet to answer the phone. They will quietly begin to recite the order of cards, starting with ace, two, three, four, and so on.

5 When they reach the correct number, say "Oh, hello."

6 They will now begin to list the suits—diamonds, spades, clubs, hearts.

7 When they reach the correct suit, say "Goodbye" and hang up.

8 Your stooge can now return to the table and correctly identify the card, to the utter astonishment of your victim!

NOTE THIS IS A REALLY GOOD TRICK IF PERFORMED PROPERLY, BUT SHOULD BE PRACTICED PROPERLY WITH A FRIEND WHO IS WILLING TO BE YOUR STOOGE.

ASHES FROM HEAVEN

YOU WILL NEED:
• some cigarette ash

THE CHALLENGE:
to perform a trick using
only cigarette ash.

METHOD:

1 Grab your participant's hands.

2 In doing so, secretly smear ash (that had been previously placed on your finger) on the palm of one of their hands.

3 Place some ashes from a lit cigarette on the back of that hand.

4 Wave your hands as a magic wand and say something suitably cheesy, such as abracadabra.

5 Blow the ash away.

6 Ask your participant to open their hand.

7 It will reveal a mysterious deposit of ash.

THE MAGIC TRIANGLE

YOU WILL NEED:
• 10 counters (you could use beer caps, coasters, or coins)

THE CHALLENGE:
to solve a geometrical riddle.

METHOD:

1 Arrange your counters in a triangle with four counters along each side.

2 Challenge someone to reverse the direction of the triangle by moving only three counters. Give them five minutes to solve the problem.

3 The solution is laid out below, and involves moving the three counters at the corners of the triangle into their new positions, creating an inverted triangle!

THE MAGIC CROSS

YOU WILL NEED:
• six counters (you could use beer caps, coasters, or coins)

THE CHALLENGE:
to solve a geometrical riddle.

METHOD:

1 Arrange the six counters to make a cross, four counters long and three counters across.

2 Challenge someone to make two rows of four by moving only one counter!

3 Set a time limit of three minutes.

SOLUTION SIMPLY TAKE THE COUNTER FROM THE BOTTOM OF THE CROSS AND PLACE IT ON TOP OF THE MIDDLE COUNTER. YOU NOW HAVE YOUR TWO ROWS OF FOUR!

SMOKE ON THE WATER

YOU WILL NEED:
• one glass
• a matchbook
• six quarters
• an ashtray
• a glass of water

THE CHALLENGE:
to get the water out of the ashtray using only the objects mentioned, and without moving or tilting the ashtray.

METHOD:

1 Fill the ashtray with a quarter inch of water.

2 Stack the quarters in the center of the ashtray so the top two quarters are above the water level.

3 Place four unlit matches on top of the quarters.

4 Light the matches.

5 Immediately cover the flame and quarters with the glass.

6 The water will be drawn into the glass and out of the ashtray!

BLOW THE BOTTLE

YOU WILL NEED:
• **one empty beer bottle and a paper napkin**

THE CHALLENGE:
to blow a napkin into a bottle.

METHOD:

1 Hold an empty beer bottle horizontally, making sure that the inside of the neck is dry.

2 Tear off a small piece of the napkin and screw it up into a small ball.

3 Place the ball just inside the lip of the bottle.

4 Hold the bottle in front of your participant's face, and bet them a drink that they cannot blow the napkin into the bottle.

5 The harder they blow, the faster the napkin will come out!

! HOW IT WORKS MOVING AIR HAS LOWER PRESSURE THAN STILL AIR. THEREFORE, WHEN YOUR PARTICIPANT BLOWS, THE STILL AIR IN THE BOTTLE WILL PUSH THE NAPKIN OUT OF THE BOTTLE.

ROLL OUT A DOLLAR

YOU WILL NEED:
• a longneck beer bottle
• a dollar bill

THE CHALLENGE:
to get a dollar bill out from underneath an upturned beer bottle without knocking over the bottle or touching it in any way.

METHOD:

1 Turn an empty bottle upside down on top of any bill.

2 Give your challengers five minutes to try the trick themselves.

3 Most people will try to pull the bill quickly out from underneath the bottle. (This will work if the bottle is completely dry and is standing on a smooth surface, so ensure the bill gets a little wet from the last few drops of beer left in the bottle.)

4 When they have given up, roll up the bill carefully up against the side of the bottle and continue rolling it against the bottle. The bottle will slide off with ease.

THE INVISIBLE HAIR

YOU WILL NEED:
- a box of matches
- a gullible participant

THE CHALLENGE:
to snap a match in two using only the "Dark Arts."

METHOD:

1 Light a match and let it burn down as far as possible without toasting your fingers.

2 Hold it carefully between forefinger and thumb, with the fingernail of your middle finger slyly hooked under the bottom of the match.

3 Tell the participant that you are going to pluck a "magic hair" from their head.

4 Pretend to do this and wrap it around the match.

5 With your free hand, pull hard on the invisible hair.

6 At the same time, flick the bottom of the match with your middle finger.

7 The head of the match will fly off dramatically!

NOTE WITH PRACTICE, THIS TRICK CAN BE SURPRISINGLY EFFECTIVE, BUT IT SHOULD NOT BE REPEATED!

THE MAGIC PALM TRICK

YOU WILL NEED:
• a glass of Sambuca

THE CHALLENGE:
to pick up the glass with one hand, but without using your fingers.

METHOD:

1 Take a match and light the Sambuca.

2 Place the palm of your hand over the glass.

3 As the flame uses all of the oxygen, it will create enough suction for you to be able to pick up the glass and wave it around in the air.

4 You should even be able to hold the glass upside down (but don't blame me if it spills everywhere).

NOTE BE CONFIDENT WHEN PLACING YOUR HAND OVER THE FLAME. HESITATE, AND YOU MAY END UP AN UNWITTING MEMBER OF THE RED HAND GANG!

THE OLD MAN'S BACK

YOU WILL NEED:
- a book of cardboard matches
- a pen

THE CHALLENGE:
to get a match to land on its side.

METHOD:

1 Take a match from the book and write H (for heads) on one side and T (for tails) on the other.

2 Tell a bar guest that you will toss the match in the air. If it lands either heads or tails you will buy him/her a drink. Should it land on its side, however, they must buy you one.

3 Once that's agreed, bend it just before you toss it in the air.

4 The match will always land on its side, earning you a free drink.

SHAVE THE FAT PENGUIN

YOU WILL NEED:
• five coins
• a stooge

THE CHALLENGE:
to demonstrate the art of "Remote Sensing."

METHOD:

1 Line up the five coins on the table and number them one to five.

2 Ensure your stooge is sitting opposite you.

3 Turn around so you can't see the coins.

4 Get your participant to point at any coin.

5 While you don't know which coin it was, your stooge does, and subtly informs you by placing the correct number of fingers on the edge of the table in a discreet manner.

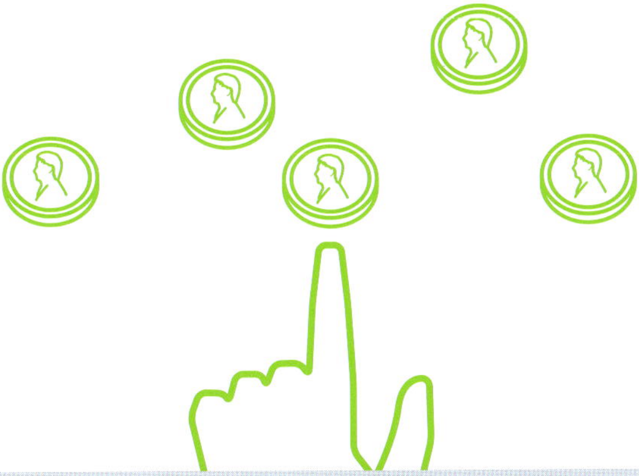

NOTE THIS TRICK CAN BE REPEATED ENDLESSLY, AND WILL HAVE YOUR VICTIM CONFUSED FOR HOURS!

THE BOURBON CHALLENGE

YOU WILL NEED:
- two identical shot glasses (one full to the brim with water, one containing a shot of bourbon)
- a non-porous piece of paper (a playing card, over-sized matchbook, or driving license will do)

THE CHALLENGE:
to get the bourbon and water into each other's glass without using any containers, including your mouth (or anyone else's mouth).

METHOD:

1 Place the non-porous piece of paper on top of the glass of water.

2 Turn the card and water shot upside down carefully. The paper should stay attached of its own accord.

3 Place the water shot glass and card on the shot of bourbon.

4 Carefully pull the paper out far enough to make a tiny opening between the two glasses.

5 The water, being heavier than alcohol, will flow into the bourbon glass and displace the bourbon up into the water glass.

X-STATIC

YOU WILL NEED:
- a box of matches
- a gullible participant

THE CHALLENGE:
to get your gullible friends to believe that static electricity can make a match jump in the air.

METHOD:

1 Balance a match on the edge of a matchbox, with the head hanging over the side.

2 Hold another match in your hand between forefinger and thumb

3 Tuck the fingernail of your middle finger discreetly under the bottom of the match.

4 Tell your friend you are going to "demonstrate the power of static electricity."

5 Rub the match into your hair "to collect static electricity."

6 Slowly move your match toward the one balanced on the box.

7 When close enough, discreetly flick the match (you are holding) with your middle fingernail, and the other match will dramatically fly up in the air.

8 Challenge your friend to do the same.

NOTE WITH PRACTICE THIS WILL WORK VERY WELL, AND IT'S HIGHLY ENTERTAINING WATCHING OTHER PEOPLE FURIOUSLY RUBBING MATCHES INTO THEIR HAIR, SWEATERS, AND BEARDS IN AN EFFORT TO MAKE THAT MATCH JUMP!

EVERLASTING ASH

YOU WILL NEED:
- a packet of cigarettes
- a paper clip

THE CHALLENGE:
to see who can smoke a cigarette the longest
without losing any ash.

METHOD:

1 In advance, straighten out the paper clip and carefully slide it down the center of your cigarette.

2 Dig it into the filter to give it some stability. If necessary, snip off the end of the clip so that it is hidden from view.

3 When the cigarette is lit and smoked, it should look completely normal, and the ash will stay on the cigarette.

VINEGAR VINCENT

YOU WILL NEED:
• a dry beer bottle
• a wall

THE CHALLENGE:
to freak people out by sticking a beer bottle to a wall without glue or bubblegum.

METHOD:

1 Walk over to a corner of the bar.

2 Place the empty beer bottle in the corner ensuring that each wall is flush with the bottle.

3 Rub the bottle gently in an up and down motion with very short strokes, making sure that the bottle doesn't move more than an inch and a half in either direction.

4 You should feel friction causing the bottle to move in shorter movements. When the bottle doesn't move in either direction, gently let go.

5 The bottle should remain "stuck" to the wall for a few seconds, or even minutes.

NOTE THIS BAR TRICK WILL NOT WORK ON ALL WALL SURFACES. DRYWALL IS GENERALLY A GOOD SURFACE, BUT YOU CAN'T GUARANTEE IT.

THE FLOATING BEER CAN

YOU WILL NEED:
- a soda or beer can
- slightly greasy fingers

THE CHALLENGE:
to make a beer can appear to be floating in the air.

METHOD:

1 Hold the can aloft in your hand, thumb on one side, fingers on the other (toward the bottom of the can).

2 Slowly release your grip. As you do so, the can will start to slide downward.

3 Move your hand upward at the same speed that the can is moving downward. If the timing is right it can create a very good illusion of the can being suspended in midair.

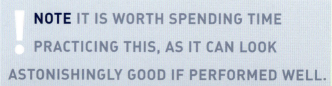

NOTE IT IS WORTH SPENDING TIME PRACTICING THIS, AS IT CAN LOOK ASTONISHINGLY GOOD IF PERFORMED WELL.

MAGNETIC MATCHES

YOU WILL NEED:
• a box of matches
• one match slightly shortened

THE CHALLENGE:
to make a box of matches magically fall to the floor.

METHOD:

1 Prepare a box of matches by inserting a shortened match width-ways in the box, on top of all the other matches but not so that it is squashing them.

2 Find a gullible participant and pull out your "magnetic matchbox."

3 Open it a quarter of the way to show the heads of the matches, shake them around to show they are loose, then close the matchbox.

4 Turn the matchbox over and wave your hand over it, in order to "magnetize the matches!"

5 Now open the box fully upside down, holding the sides of the box lightly between two fingers to ensure that your shortened match stays in place and the matches do not fall.

6 With a quick shift of the hand (i.e. squeezing the ends of the box), "de-magnetize" the matchbox and the matches will fall to the ground, to the bemusement of your guest.

RISING BEER BOTTLE TRICK

YOU WILL NEED:
- a dry, empty beer bottle with a flat bottom
- a leather belt

THE CHALLENGE:
to pick up an upturned beer bottle with just the palm of your hand.

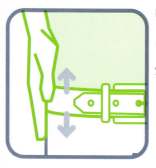

METHOD:

1 Discreetly rub your thumb and fingers up and down your leather belt several times.

2 Place the empty bottle upside down on the table.

3 Place your thumb against the side of the bottle with your fingers over the bottom.

4 Form a right angle with your thumb and first finger.

5 Slowly pick up the bottle without touching it with your other fingers or anything else.

! NOTE THIS SHOULD PROVE DIFFICULT FOR YOUR PEERS TO MASTER, ESPECIALLY IF THEIR BOTTLE IS WET.

ROLL ME A CIGARETTE

YOU WILL NEED:
• a straw or cigarette

THE CHALLENGE:
to move a cigarette around the table without touching it.

METHOD:

1 Lay a cigarette on a table and explain that you are about to hypnotize it.

2 Put your face a little closer to the cigarette as if concentrating on it and place your hand behind, as if about to pull it on an imaginary thread.

3 Blow lightly on the cigarette.

4 As it moves, pull your hand back to make it look as if the hand is pulling the cigarette.

5 To further baffle your audience, cup the hand that is behind the cigarette and, if you blow gently against that hand, the cigarette will roll back toward you.

6 For a grand finale, discreetly draw a small wet line on the table and you can even command the cigarette to stop dead by blowing it into the wet patch.

NOTE THIS SIMPLE TRICK WILL FOOL MANY PEOPLE. DON'T WORRY ABOUT THEM DISCOVERING YOU BLOWING, AS THE NOISE IN THE BAR SHOULD MAKE SURE THEY DON'T HEAR YOU.

BUM FLICK

YOU WILL NEED:
- **a packet of cigarettes**
- **a full bottle of beer**
- **a beer mat**
- **a fast pair of running shoes**

THE CHALLENGE:
to get rid of an unwelcome drunk by getting him to spill beer down himself.

METHOD:

1 Wait until your unwanted guest has gone to the bathroom and left his bottle of beer behind.

2 Take the plastic wrapper off a cigarette packet and cut a small disk from it with a lit cigarette, big enough to cover the mouth of the bottle.

3 Wet the rim and carefully stick the plastic circle on top of the bottle.

4 Place a beer mat on top of the bottle, hold it in place and then turn the bottle upside down.

5 Remove the beer mat carefully (the plastic should keep the beer inside the bottle), and leave the bottle upside down on the bar.

6 When your unwelcome guest returns, he will undoubtedly be baffled as to how his bottle came to be upside down without any beer being spilled.

7 Pick up the bottle and hand it to him (the plastic, if it has been stuck down properly, should still hold the beer in place).

8 As he takes it from you, tap the bottom of the "magic" bottle gently (or simply flick off the plastic) and run.

PUSH A DOLLAR THROUGH A LEMON

YOU WILL NEED:
• a ripe lemon
• a dollar bill

THE CHALLENGE:
to pass a dollar
through a lemon.

METHOD:

1 Fold one corner of the
dollar bill down to the
opposite side of the bill at
45° to make a sharp point.

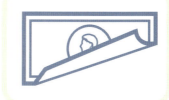

2 Tightly roll the bill up,
starting at the long side
so that the point protrudes
from the middle of the rolled
bill, and keeping the point
nice and sharp.

3 Insert the dollar into
the lemon, point first,
twisting in the direction that
keeps the bill tightly rolled,
and pushing as you do so.

4 The bill should pass
through the lemon
with relative ease, much
to astonishment of the
onlookers!

THE VANISHING CIGARETTE

YOU WILL NEED:
• a cigarette

THE CHALLENGE:
to make a cigarette
magically disappear.

METHOD:

1 Lick your thumb just below
the nail.

2 Push the non-filter end of the
cigarette against your wet
thumb and index finger.

3 Offer the cigarette to
someone.

4 As they reach to take it,
quickly open your hand so
the cigarette becomes hidden
behind your thumb.

5 To their astonishment, it will
have completely disappeared.

NOTE THIS NEEDS A LOT OF PRACTICE
BEFORE LOOKING TRULY IMPRESSIVE.
TRY IT IN FRONT OF A MIRROR!

THE HOTHEADED COIN

YOU WILL NEED:
• five different coins
• a hat

THE CHALLENGE:
to pick the coin selected from the hat.

METHOD:

1 Place the coins in the hat.

2 Get someone to pick one out and hold it to his or her forehead for 15 seconds for everyone else to see, while you turn away.

3 Ask them to replace the coin in the hat.

4 Reach into the hat, close your eyes, say a magic incantation, and simply pick out the warmest coin!

NOTE IT WILL TAKE A FEW MOMENTS TOUCHING THE COINS TO ASCERTAIN WHICH IS THE WARMEST. USE THIS TIME TO PRETEND YOU ARE PICKING UP THE "AURA" THE PERSON HAS LEFT ON THE COIN (OR SOME SUCH BALONEY).

|||||| EAT MY MIRKIN

YOU WILL NEED:
• six matches

THE CHALLENGE:
to make four equilateral triangles
out of six matches, without breaking any!

METHOD:

1 Give your participant(s) five minutes to try and solve this conundrum.

2 Once your participants have given up, simply construct a three-sided pyramid, holding it in place with your fingers and thumbs!

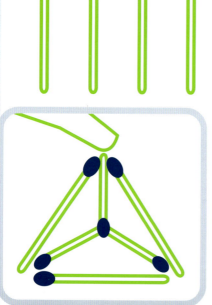

⊘ QUARTER FALLS

YOU WILL NEED:
• a quarter

THE CHALLENGE:
to predict the side of a coin that lands face up when spun.

METHOD:

1 Stand the quarter upright on the table.

2 Make a mental note of which side of the coin is facing you.

3 Using your index finger, spin the coin.

4 Before the coin stops spinning and falls flat, make your prediction based on the face that was toward you (i.e. if heads was facing you before you spun, the coin should finish heads up).

NOTE THE COIN IS EFFECTIVELY SPINNING ON ITS BACK EDGE BECAUSE YOU HAVE FLICKED IT AWAY FROM YOU. THIS TRICK IS NOT INFALLIBLE, BUT 90% OF THE TIME YOU SHOULD BE SPOT ON— ENOUGH TO ASTOUND YOUR AUDIENCE!

rules of the game

pool/billiards

history

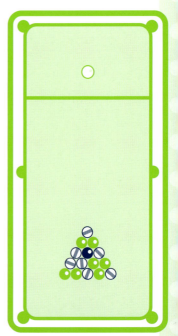

"BILLIARDS" REFERS TO ANY GAME PLAYED ON A TABLE WITH A CUE AND BALLS. ITS ORIGINS LIE WITH THE ENGLISH SPORT OF CROQUET—AN OUTDOOR GAME PLAYED ON THE LAWN WITH MALLETS (TRADITIONALLY PLAYED BY PEOPLE WITH NAMES LIKE LORD TARQUIN SMITH-SMYTHE-SMITH OR LADY PAMELA HUGHES-BYRON-ALGERNON), THE OBJECT OF WHICH IS TO KNOCK A BALL THROUGH A SERIES OF HOOPS IN A CERTAIN ORDER. ONE DAY SOME BRIGHT SPARK, FED UP WITH "RAIN STOPS PLAY" (A FAR TOO COMMON OCCURRENCE IN ENGLAND), GOT THE IDEA OF EXCHANGING THE LAWN FOR A SPECIALLY MADE TABLE WITH POCKETS INSTEAD OF HOOPS, AND SO "BILLIARDS" WAS BORN. AS THE GAME DEVELOPED, MALLETS WERE EXCHANGED FOR CUES, AND MANY DIFFERENT VARIATIONS OF THE GAME EMERGED, INCLUDING SNOOKER.

Billiards was first introduced to North America by English and Dutch settlers, and it proved to be immensely popular. By 1830, a number of public rooms had opened up around the country, entirely devoted to the game. The name "pool" came about in the days when billiard tables were installed in gambling houses to keep the customers occupied between horse races. Naturally, they liked to gamble when playing, and before each game would make a collective bet known as a "pool" (as in a "pool of money") and the name stuck.

   Although pool houses had almost became extinct by the 1950s, the game experienced a remarkable revival in the 1960s, thanks, in no small part, to the popularity of the Paul Newman film *The Hustler* (and, in the 80s, *The Color of Money*), and pool remains today one of the most popular bar games around the world.

the games

8-BALL

The most popular billiards game in the US, 8-ball uses 15 numbered balls and a cue ball. Two players are each allocated balls 1–7 and 9–15, and must attempt to pocket their seven balls as quickly as possible. The player pocketing his balls first and then legally pocketing the 8-ball in a specific pocket wins the game.

9-BALL

A short and simple game, using just the first nine numbered balls. The balls are racked in a diamond shape, with the 1-ball at the top of the diamond, the 9-ball in the center, and the rest in random order. For each shot, the first ball the white contacts must be the lowest-numbered ball on the table, though the balls need not be pocketed in order. A player may remain on the table for another go if he or she pockets a ball on a legal shot. Whoever pockets the 9-ball is the winner.

14.1 (OR STRAIGHT POOL)

Played with 15 numbered balls and a cue ball, 14.1 is a nomination game, with each player having to nominate the ball and the pocket he is going to sink it in each time. If accomplished, the player may continue until he or she misses or fouls. When only one ball remains on the table, the other 14 are racked up again and the player who pocketed the 14th attempts to pocket the 15th ball such that the newly-racked 14 are disturbed and he or she can continue his run. A point is scored for each ball correctly pocketed and the first player to make 150 is the winner.

FACT HAVING BOTH FEET OFF THE FLOOR TO TAKE A SHOT IS CONSIDERED ILLEGAL IN POOL. THERE HAVE, HOWEVER, BEEN RARE EXCEPTIONS TO THIS RULE IN PROFESSIONAL GAMES: THE LATE GREAT WILLIE MOSCONI, WHEN COMPETING AS A BOY, HAD SUCH SHORT LEGS THAT HE WAS PERMITTED TO STAND ON A BOX WHILE ATTEMPTING TO TAKE CERTAIN SHOTS!

darts

history

FOR A GAME VERY MUCH ASSOCIATED WITH PORTLY MEN WITH BAD HAIR, BEER BELLIES, AND A 20-A-DAY HABIT, IT IS IRONIC THAT THE GAME OF DARTS ACTUALLY BEGAN AS A FORM OF MARTIAL ARTS TRAINING IN MEDIEVAL ENGLAND. IN THE DAYS WHEN GUYS WOULD SPEND A FAIR AMOUNT OF THEIR TIME FIGHTING DRAGONS AND RESCUING DAMSELS FROM THE CLUTCHES OF GIANTS, THE IMPORTANCE OF GOOD ARCHERY SKILLS WAS PARAMOUNT, AND THROWING SHORTENED ARROWS AT THE BOTTOM OF AN EMPTY WINE BARREL WAS ONE WAY TO PRACTICE THEIR AIM. THE EMPTY BARREL WAS SOON REPLACED BY THE CROSS-SECTION OF A MODERATE-SIZED TREE. WITH ITS SIZE, CIRCULAR FRAME, AND NATURAL RINGS, IT IS EASY TO SEE HOW THE MODERN DARTBOARD DEVELOPED FROM THIS. GAMES SOON DEVELOPED USING THESE SHORTENED ARROWS AND A SIMPLE BOARD, AND IT WASN'T LONG BEFORE EVERYONE IN ENGLAND WAS HAVING FUN THROWING DARTS AROUND. HENRY VIII BECAME SO PARTIAL TO THE GAME THAT HE HAD AN ORNATE BOARD MADE FOR HIS WIFE, ANNE BOLEYN, AS A WEDDING GIFT, SHORTLY BEFORE CHOPPING HER HEAD OFF.

During the 1800s and early 1900s, when the sexually-repressed, tea-drinking Brits felt they really owed it to the "uncivilized world" to make it their empire, darts' popularity spread worldwide, and by 1900 the size of the board, throwing distance, and rules of the game had become the standard we still know today.

Darts remains one of the all-time perfect bar games: it is sociable, requires minimum physical effort, and somehow makes beer taste better. What more do you need to score a bullseye?

HOW TO PLAY KILLER

The most popular darts game in the world is 301. Killer, however, is a game that turns ordinary decent people into highly competitive, scheming, and mistrustful cads, and is, therefore, the best darts game ever invented. It can be played with as few or as many players as you can reasonably fit around a dartboard. A good game of Killer, if played properly, can end life-long friendships, start fights, and destroy marriages, as it inevitably involves ganging up on people who once considered you their friend, and making promises to other "friends" that you will instantly break the next time it's your turn to throw.

1 Each player throws a dart at the board with their non-throwing hand. The number they hit becomes their number.

2 The players' names and numbers are written on a blackboard.

3 Players take it in turns, using three darts each go, to hit their own number. Each hit scores as one letter in the word, KILLER, to be written on the blackboard.

4 Players continue aiming at their own number until they have had six hits, completing the word, so that KILLER now appears below their name.

5 A player whose number is hit by a player who is not a KILLER receives a letter.

6 Once a player is a KILLER, he or she can start killing other players by aiming for their number. Each correct hit eliminates a letter from that player.

7 Any player who loses all of his letters through being killed, is eliminated from the game.

8 If a person who is a KILLER loses a letter from his word by being killed by someone else (i.e. another KILLER lands a dart in his number), he cannot continue as a KILLER, until he has replaced the missing letter/s by again hitting his own number.

9 Doubles and triples count as two and three letters respectively.

10 The last remaining player on the board is the winner.

foosball/
table soccer

history

BASED (VERY LOOSELY!) ON THE ENGLISH GAME OF SOCCER, FOOSBALL FIRST ORIGINATED IN GERMANY IN THE 1920S. THE GERMANS, BEING AS SOCCER CRAZY AS THE BRITS, HAD SOCCER TEAMS IN VIRTUALLY EVERY VILLAGE IN THE COUNTRY AND WOULD REGULARLY CONGREGATE IN THE BARS AFTER A MATCH TO SUP GOOD BEER AND ANALYZE THE GAME. IT WAS ALMOST INEVITABLE, THEREFORE, THAT SOME ENTERPRISING SOUL WOULD COME UP WITH A WAY OF CONTINUING THE MATCH IN THE BAR, AND FOOSBALL WAS THE SOLUTION. ITS FIRST INCARNATION WAS QUITE CRUDE, WITH WOODEN DOWELS FOR RODS, PLAIN RECTANGULAR BLOCKS OF WOOD FOR THE PLAYERS, AND A RECTANGULAR PLYWOOD BOX FOR THE TABLE, BUT IT PROVED TO BE IMMENSE FUN, ENJOYED BY YOUNG AND OLD ALIKE, AND IT WASN'T LONG BEFORE TABLES WERE BEING CONSTRUCTED BY LOCAL CARPENTERS AND MEMBERS OF OTHER SOCCER TEAMS THE LENGTH AND BREADTH OF THE COUNTRY.

After World War II, Germany tried to export the game to the US but with little success; the game of soccer was still relatively unknown to North Americans then. It wasn't until the 1960s, when Foosball became popular with the US armed forces based in Europe, that the games began to be sold in ever-growing numbers to the US Army. With over a quarter of a million US servicemen returning home each year, the game's popularity soon spread directly back to the US. Now, along with the flipper, shuffle, and pool table, Foosball enjoys cult status in bars, pubs, and cafés the world over.

FACT ANOTHER VARIATION ON THE FOOSBALL IDEA IS SUBBUTEO, A GAME INVOLVING FREESTANDING PLASTIC FIGURES WHO ARE FLICKED WITH THE FINGERTIPS TO MOVE THEM AROUND THE PITCH.

HOW TO PLAY

There can be as few or as many rules for Foosball as you like. Most people just like to throw the ball in and away they go. Here are a few rules of my own that you can adhere to or ignore at your leisure.

1 Should the ball gets stuck in a no-man's-land where neither team can reach it, violent shaking or lifting of the table is permitted by whichever team takes the initiative first.

2 If the ball goes off the table, it has to be thrown back in by a random passer-by.

3 For a goal to be permitted, the ball must have touched at least one player from both teams first.

4 If the table is glass-topped, players must swap sides each game, in case harsh light reflection on the glass disadvantages play on one of the sides.

5 No spinning.

6 No cursing.

7 No animals allowed on the pitch.

8 Smoking and drinking are compulsory.

poker

history

POKER IS A MACHISMO GAME OF INTIMACY, STYLE, COURAGE, AND BLUFF. IT IS ALSO THE WORLD'S MOST CELEBRATED AND POPULAR CARD GAME, AND, THOUGH RESTRICTED NOWADAYS TO CASINOS AND CARDROOMS, IT STILL EVOKES ROMANTIC IMAGES OF SEEDY SALOONS IN THE WILD WEST, WITH LEATHER-FACED MEN GAMBLING AWAY THEIR HORSES, HOUSES, WIVES, AND CHILDREN, AND OCCASIONALLY SHOOTING EACH OTHER FOR GOOD MEASURE.

The first reference to poker dates back to 1834, when a Mr Jonathan H. Green described it as "a gambling game for two to four players being dealt five cards each." He went on, however, to describe it as a "cheating game." Like three-card Monte and other classic card tricks, it seems that poker was originally used by cardsharps to cheat people out of their money on Mississippi riverboats.

The origin of the name has been the subject of much debate over the years. Depending which version you believe, poker got its name from either the old magician's catch-phrase "hocus-pocus," the Hindu word "pukka," or even the French and German card games of "poque" and "Pochspeil" respectively. The most likely explanation, however, is that it originated from the underworld slang term "poke," meaning to pickpocket.

While no longer permitted as a bar game, poker's synonymy with alcohol remains complete. It is, and always should be, a game that demands hard drinking, chain smoking, and all-round liver abuse. To spend an intimate night with friends, gambling, knocking back the whiskey, and bingeing on snacks in a smoke-filled room, remains one of life's greatest pleasures, if one of the most potentially expensive!

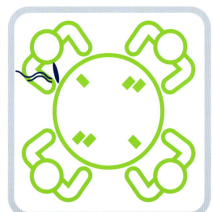

the rules of the game

- **Poker is played with a standard pack of 52 cards.**

- **The cards are ranked (from low to high) A, 2, 3, 4, 5, 6, 7, 8, 9, 10, J, Q, K, A (the Ace can be low or high, but is usually high).**

- **No suit is deemed higher than any other.**

ORDER OF PLAY

1 Players place the "ante" (see page 116) in the center of the table.

2 Each player is dealt five cards, face down.

3 Players bet on their hands until everyone has either matched or folded.

4 Each player may then, in turn, choose to exchange one, two, three, four, or even all five of their cards with the dealer.

5 Betting resumes until everyone either calls or folds after a raise or initial bet.

6 In the event of a call (or showdown), remaining players must show their cards, and the one with the highest hand wins the pot. If everyone folds, the last remaining player automatically wins the pot and does not have to show his hand.

HANDS ARE RANKED AS FOLLOWS
(from low to high)

High Card
if no one has a pair or better, the highest card wins, with Ace being the highest.

A Pair
two cards of equal value e.g. 6-6.

Two Pairs
e.g. Q-Q, 5-5.

Three of a Kind
e.g. K-K-K.

A Straight
a run of cards in order (such as 5-6-7-8-9), but the cards may be of different suits.

A Flush
all the cards are of the same suit, e.g. J-8-5-3-K of spades.

A Full House
three of a kind and a pair, e.g. K-K-K-5-5.

Four of a Kind
e.g. 7-7-7-7.

A Straight Flush
a run of cards in order (such as 9-10-J-Q-K), but the cards must all be of the same suit.

poker terminology

ANTE: This is a fixed amount of money with which to participate in the game. It could be 10 cents or $1,000 depending on how poor or obscenely rich you are.

CHECK: A player says check when he or she wishes to stay in play but does not wish to make a bet. A player can only check if they are leading the betting or if no bet has yet been placed on the table.

CALL/MATCH: This is when a player equals the bet set by other players. For example, if one player bets a dime, all other players must match that to stay in play. If one player matches the dime and another raises by a quarter before it is your turn again, you would then need to put in 35 cents to match the bet.

RAISE: Once a player has matched a bet, he or she may also raise it by the fixed amount agreed by the table. If you bet a dime and the bet has been raised to a quarter, the next time you bet you will need to add 15 cents to match and more to raise.

FOLD: When a player wishes to leave the game, he or she must fold and place their cards face down on the table, or return them to the dealer. A player may fold at any time during the game, but only when it is their turn to play. Once having folded, a player does not need to add any more money to the pot.

STAKE: The agreed amount of money for the betting. It is wise to have an upper limit to the stake, unless you have a Bill Gates-sized bank account. For example, you could set the ante at 50 cents, minimum bet 50 cents, maximum $2.

HOW TO BET

Betting should start with a different player each game, beginning with the player on the dealer's left.

The first person to bet must place an initial bet, check, or fold.

Once a bet has been placed, the rest of the players must either match the bet (to stay in the game), or raise.

If a player lays a bet that is matched but not raised, that same player cannot make another raise. The betting is over.

Betting continues until everyone has matched the bet or folded.

texas hold 'em

Texas Hold 'Em (or Holdem) is the version of poker played in many casinos, and seen on the Travel Channel's *World Poker Tour* and ESPN's *World Series of Poker*. These are the basic rules.

The Shuffle, The Deal, The Blinds

The dealer shuffles a standard 52-card deck. (In casinos, the dealer never plays. A round disc—known as the "dealer button"—moves clockwise from player to player with each hand to mark which player would be the dealer if the deal were advanced from player to player.)

Most Texas Hold 'Em Poker games start with the two players to the left of the dealer (the button) putting a fixed amount of money into the pot before any cards are dealt, ensuring that there's something to play for on every hand. This is called "posting the blinds."

Each player is then dealt two cards, face down. These are the "hole cards."

Betting Begins

A round of betting takes place, beginning with the player to the left of the two who posted the blinds. Players can call, raise, or fold when it's their turn to bet.

The Flop

After the first betting round, the dealer discards (or "burns") the top card of the deck, in case anyone accidentally saw the top card, and to prevent cheating.

The dealer then flips the next three cards face up on the table. These cards—the "flop"—are the first three of a total of five community cards that will be placed face up on the table. Players can use any combination of these community cards and their own two hole cards to form the best possible five-card poker hand.

After the flop, another round of betting takes place, beginning with the player to the left of the dealer (the button). During this round of betting and the rounds that follow, each player can check, call, raise, or fold when it's his or her turn to bet.

Fourth Street

The dealer "burns" another card and plays one more face up onto the table. This, the fourth community card, is called the "turn" or "Fourth Street."

The third round of betting is started by the player to the left of the button.

Fifth Street

The dealer burns another card before placing the final face-up card on the table. This card is called the "river" or "Fifth Street."

Final Betting and The Winner

Players can now use any combination of seven cards—the five community cards and their own two hole cards that only they have seen—to form the best possible five-card poker hand.

The fourth and final round of betting starts with the player to the left of the dealer (the button).

Once the final round of betting has been completed, all the players who remain in the game reveal their hands. The player who made the initial bet or the one who made the last raise shows his or her hand first.

The player with the best hand wins.

dominoes

history

DOMINOES ARE SMALL BLACK AND WHITE NUMBERED TILES THAT ORIGINATED IN CHINA. THEY ARE KNOWN TO HAVE EVOLVED IN SOME WAY FROM CUBIC DICE, AS EACH TILE IN A DOMINO SET REPRESENTS ONE OF THE 21 RESULTS OF THROWING TWO DICE (ONE AND ONE, TWO AND ONE, THREE AND ONE ETC.). THESE TILES EVOLVED OVER TIME INTO THE GAME KNOWN AS MAH JONG, WHICH BECAME IMMENSELY POPULAR IN THE US DURING THE 1920S. IN EUROPE AND THE WEST, THE 28-TILE SET DEVELOPED, WHICH INCLUDES SEVEN EXTRA TILES (SIX OF THEM COMBINING A BLANK AND ONE OF THE NUMBERS FROM ONE TO SIX, AND A DOUBLE BLANK).

The game may have come to England from France, and the name of the game itself may have French origins, the French word *domino* being the term for a Christian priest's winter hood that was black on the outside, white on the inside. It also happens to be the name of a very cool record label.

Dominoes is still immensely popular in different corners of the world, played in the streets and cafés of such far-flung countries as Cuba and the Netherlands. In the UK, it is still traditionally played in pubs by very old men with hairy ears, sporting flat caps, and all called Stanley.

There is a plethora of games you can play with dominoes. It can be as meditative as chess, as noisy as table soccer, or as aggressive as football (well, almost). Different versions include 42 (a trick-taking game, popular in Texas), Longana (recently popularized by the film *Buena Vista Social Club*), and Chickenfoot. One of the most popular styles worldwide–and the simplest to learn–is Draw (a.k.a. "Muggins," "Five-Up," or simply "Dominoes"), the rules of which are described opposite.

HOW TO PLAY

- Place the 28 tiles face-down on the table and shuffle them around.

- Take seven tiles each and allow the person with the highest double (or, failing that, highest total) to go first. (If three or four players are involved, take five dominoes each instead of seven.)

- Place a domino with the same number value next to the first domino (e.g. if the first tile was double five, you could place a five-one next to it), ensuring those of like-value are touching.

- Each player can continue taking turns at adding to the tiles on the table, provided they have a domino with a number that corresponds to those at either end of the chain.

- If you cannot go, you must pick up from the pile of remaining upturned dominoes.

- Once the spare pile of dominoes has gone, if you cannot go you must pass.

- The first person to run out of dominoes is the winner.

IF THERE'S ONE THING BETTER THAN HAVING A COLD BEER WITH A BUNCH OF FRIENDS, IT'S HAVING A COLD BEER AND WATCHING THE BIG GAME ON TV WITH A BUNCH OF FRIENDS. AND BEING ABLE TO TALK MORE DRIVEL THAN THE COMMENTATOR JUST ADDS SPICE, SO HERE ARE SOME OF THE BASICS.

hockey

OBJECTIVE
To win by scoring more goals than the opponent. This is achieved by getting the puck into the opponent's goal.

LENGTH OF THE GAME
The game lasts three equal periods of 20 minutes, but since the clock stops for any break in play, it usually takes about three hours.

NUMBER OF PLAYERS
Six in each team on the ice at any one time.

THE PUCK
The puck is a vulcanized rubber disk, 1in (2.5cm) thick, 3in (7.5cm) in diameter, and weighing 5½–6oz (156–170gm).

ODDEST RULE
Offside. A team is offside when both the skates of any member of the attacking team precede the puck over the defending team's blue line. If he has only one skate over the blue line and one on it, he is onside. The position of his stick is irrelevant.

HOCKEY FACTS
- Hockey began in Canada in the mid 1800s.
- The Stanley Cup, donated by Lord Stanley of Preston, Governor-General of Canada, in 1893, was first won by a US-based team (the Seattle Metropolitans) in 1917.
- The United States' Gold Medal win against the Soviet Union in the 1980 Winter Olympics, since immortalized in the film *Miracle*, has been called the defining moment in American hockey.

football

OBJECTIVE

To win by scoring more points than the opponent. Points can be awarded through touchdowns, field goals, or two-point conversions.

LENGTH OF GAME

Although divided into four 15-minute quarters, a typical game can take three to four hours to play, as the "clock" can stop for reasons ranging from "running out of bounds," to "throwing an incomplete pass," or "the last ever episode of *Friends*."

NUMBER OF PLAYERS

Eleven in each team.

THE BALL

An oblong sphere, 11 to 11.5in (28 to 29.2cm) long, with a cowhide covering.

ODDEST RULE

The down-and-distance system. Involving complex algebraic equations, a 10-yard-long chain, and such bizarre imaginary places as the line of scrimmage, the down-and-distance system can only really be understood by true initiates to the ancient art of alchemy, or those who have taken enough doses of psilocybin mushrooms.

FOOTBALL FACTS

- The father of American football is Yale graduate, Walter Camp, who came up with the game by making radical changes to the rules of British rugby, such as reducing the number of players in a team to 11, instead of 15.
- The first game of American football took place in 1874 when Harvard University played McGill University.
- In 1905 President Theodore Roosevelt threatened to ban college football owing to the fact that, in that year alone, 18 players died as a result of their injuries.
- The NFL began in 1920 as the American Professional Football Association, changing to its present name two years later.

baseball

OBJECTIVE

To win by scoring more runs than the opponent.

NUMBER OF PLAYERS

Nine in each team.

LENGTH OF GAME

A regulation game consists of nine innings, unless extended (because of a tie score), or shortened (because the home team needs none of its half of the ninth inning or needs only a fraction of it).

THE BALL

A tightly-stitched white leather sphere, weighing 5.25oz (150g).

ODDEST RULE

Pitchers may spit anywhere they like, except on the ball.

BASEBAL FACTS

- Baseball originated from the game rounders, a popular and simple game played on sandlots.
- The first World Series was played in 1903. It was between Pittsburgh and Boston and was a nine-game series. Boston won 5-3.
- The New York Yankees have won more World Series' titles than any other team.
- Baseball became a national obsession from the 1920s onward, due, in part, to the legendary Babe Ruth, who led the New York Yankees to several World Series' titles and became a national hero on the strength of his home runs.

basketball

OBJECTIVE
To toss the ball into the opposing team's basket and win by scoring more points.

NUMBER OF PLAYERS
Five in each team.

LENGTH OF GAME
Four 12-minute quarters (for NBA).

THE BALL
A basketball is made of leather or composite leather, and is roughly 9.4in (24cm) in diameter.

ODDEST RULE
"Over the back" foul. This is confusing, because there is actually no such foul. It is not illegal to reach over the back of another player, especially to get a rebound. It is illegal, however, to contact the player with the body while reaching over the opponent, but to be a foul you need to physically displace the opponent and it must affect the play.

BASKETBALL FACTS
- Basketball was invented in 1891 by James Naismith, a teacher at a YMCA in Springfield, Massachusetts, who had been instructed to "invent a new game to keep his disorderly class occupied."
- Before the introduction of hoops, peach baskets were originally used.
- Basketball became an official Olympic event at the Summer Games in Berlin, Germany in 1936.
- The Boston Celtics have won more NBA championships than any other team, including seven straight from 1960 to 1966.
- Michael Jordan has scored more points–5,987– in the playoffs than any other player.

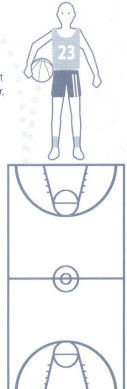

how it works

a commercial
pool table

the surface

Traditionally the surface of a pool table should be made of slate (Italian being the best) as it is a very flat stone—easily ground and polished. These days, inexpensive tables tend to be made of hard synthetic sheets of plastic or MDF (pressed wood).

Green cloth is then stretched over the slate and stapled or tacked to the frame. Although known as the felt, this material is usually a tightly-woven cloth, made primarily of wool. The cushions, made of hard rubber, are glued around the sides.

BALL RETURN

A system of chutes carries the pool balls from the pockets back to the collection chamber. Each chute is angled downward so that when a ball falls into a pocket, gravity does the rest. By placing coins in the slot at the side of the table and pushing the coin arm, a lever is triggered, allowing the balls to roll out of the collection chamber to the access area.

the cue ball

If the cue ball is accidentally pocketed during a game, it needs to be returned for the game to continue, rather than ending up in the collection chamber with all the colored balls. This problem is overcome in two ways:

1 The cue ball is oversized (by just over a sixteenth of an inch) and is therefore too big to roll down the chute to the collection chamber. Instead, it is directed down a separate chute that takes it straight back to the access area.

2 The cue ball is magnetic. When it falls down a pocket, it triggers a magnetic detector that deflects it down a separate chute. While both techniques are, unquestionably, clever ways of getting round a tricky problem, they are not without their shortcomings. Professional players often complain that magnetic cue balls lack a "true roll" and are prone to shatter easily if dropped, while oversized cue balls can feel awkward to anyone used to playing with a standard-sized cue ball.

an ice-maker

AN ICE-MAKER IS A HANDY FELLOW
WHO USUALLY LIVES INSIDE A FREEZER,
THOUGH IT NORMALLY WORKS
INDEPENDENTLY OF OTHER
REFRIGERATOR SYSTEMS.

When ice is needed, a signal is sent to a
water-fill valve to open. A fixed amount of
water then flows from a tap–usually under a
kitchen sink or behind a fridge–into the ice-
maker, controlled by an internal motor and
switch. When the water tray thermostat
senses that the tray has reached a certain
temperature, it signals the ice-maker to
begin ejecting cubes. The ice-mold is then
warmed by a heater to permit the ice to be
pushed out easily. Another motor turns the
ejector blades that push ice into the bin. A
wire (or shut-off arm) rises up while the ice
is being ejected and then drops down
again. When the ice level drops sufficiently,
the ice-maker detects this from the position
of the arm and the process begins again.

PERFECT ICE CUBES ICE IS USUALLY
CLOUDY IN THE MIDDLE. THIS IS DUE TO
IT BEING FROZEN RAPIDLY, GIVING RISE TO
TRAPPED AIR BUBBLES AND CRACKS IN
THE CENTRE. TO AVOID THIS, EITHER
FREEZE YOUR WATER VERY, VERY SLOWLY–
GIVING RISE TO PERFECTLY CLEAR ICE–OR
GET YOUR ICE DIRECT FROM ANTARCTICA.

a neon light

A NEON LIGHT IS A LONG, NARROW TUBE OF GLASS FILLED WITH LOW-PRESSURE GAS (USUALLY NEON, THOUGH ARGON OR KRYPTON CAN ALSO BE USED).

At each end of the tube is a metal electrode. When a high voltage is applied across these electrodes, the gas ionizes and electrons flow through the tube. The neon atoms, aroused by all these electrons whizzing around, get all excited and begin to emit light. If the gas inside is neon, the light will be red (other gases emit different colors). For those unsure of the difference between neon and fluorescent lights, neon lights are often bent into shapes to spell words (such as "Budweiser"), while fluorescent strip lights are those nasty things that they put up in offices and superstores to make everyone look more haggard and pale than they really are.

! FACT THE BASIC PRINCIPLES BEHIND CREATING A NEON SIGN HAD BEEN NOTED AS EARLY AS 1675, WHEN FRENCH ASTRONOMER JEAN PICARD OBSERVED A FAINT GLOW IN A MERCURY BAROMETER TUBE WHEN IT WAS SHAKEN!

a one-armed bandit

DESPITE THE VAST ARRAY OF AVAILABLE SOPHISTICATED GAMBLING MACHINES IN WHICH TO THROW AWAY YOUR HARD-EARNED MONEY, THE MECHANICALLY-OPERATED ONE-ARMED BANDIT REMAINS AN ENDURING CLASSIC. IT OPERATES USING A COMPLEX CONFIGURATION OF GEARS AND LEVERS.

When a detector registers that a coin has been inserted, the central metal shaft, which supports the reels and is connected to the handle, gets the reels spinning. Brakes then slow the reels, and a series of teeth lock into the three reels, stopping them one at a time (purely for the sake of suspense). Sensors then communicate the position of the reels to the payout system.

Much has changed, however, since the first days of this simple, yet brilliant, design. In modern slot machines, the outcome of each pull is now controlled by a central computer inside the machine, with manufacturers being able to configure how often a machine pays out (how "loose" or "tight" it is). The odds of hitting the jackpot image on all three reels of a typical slot-machine are 1:643.

Each machine, however, is designed to achieve a certain payback percentage. While the law requires that payback percentages must be no lower than 75 percent (i.e. 75 percent of all the money put into the machine must be returned to those using it), many companies, not wanting their machines to be seen as "tighter" than the competitors, usually set their payback percentages at between 90 and 97 percent. Although this may seem an incredibly low profit margin, rest assured that the odds of losing all your cash in these machines remain firmly in the owner's favor.

POPULAR MYTHS

One-armed bandits can be instantly "tightened up" to ensure fewer payouts.
Not true: the odds for slot machines are usually programmed into the machine and cannot be changed without replacing this computer chip.

A machine can be "ready to pay."
Not true: you have exactly the same chance of winning the jackpot on the same machine each time you play, regardless of how long you have been playing, as a random number generator in the computer ensures that each pull has an equal chance of winning the jackpot.

drinking games

drinking games

EVERYONE'S PLAYED THEM, AND NO DOUBT EVERYONE'S REGRETTED IT, BUT IT DOESN'T STOP US DOING IT AGAIN, SO HERE ARE A FEW CLASSIC DRINKING GAMES TO REMIND YOU. AFTER A FEW DRINKS YOU'LL REMEMBER THE RULES ANYWAY! THE POSSIBILITIES ARE ENDLESS, SO LOOK AROUND ON THE WEB TO ADD TO YOUR REPERTOIRE.

drop the cent

A Kleenex is secured over a full glass of beer and a coin is placed on top. Players have to take turns burning holes in the paper with a lighted cigarette, and the one who causes the coin to fall through has to sink the brew (being careful not to swallow the cent). This works well—if not a little better—with the carefully peeled top layer of a paper coaster.

truth, dare, or drink

This game involves flipping and calling a coin. If you're wrong, you must choose between Truth (revealing an embarrassing fact in a category thought up by the other players), Dare (doing something stupid in public), or Drink (downing a double of your favorite beverage), though you can't do the same thing more than twice in a row. This game provides a great opportunity to learn a few scandalous facts/ lies about your friends.

speed quarters

You'll need beer, people (6 is good), two glasses, and two quarters. Sit everyone in a circle, and give a quarter and a glass to two people sitting more or less opposite each other in the circle. On the word "GO!" they try to bounce their quarters into the glass. They keep trying for as long as it takes, and when each person succeeds, that person then passes the quarter and the glass to the person on their left. Then this person must bounce the quarter in. This goes on until a glass catches up to a person who already has a glass. This person then must drink some beer. You choose the amount, or start with a beer in the middle of the table that must be drunk.

the sentence game

Each player mentions one word in turn; the words should keep forming a proper sentence. The player who either renders the sentence gibberish or completes it must drink three fingers of spirits.

I have never...

Each person takes it in turns to make a statement about something they have never done, e.g. I have never stolen anything/shaved my pubic hair/drunk my own urine etc. If anyone has done this (and the game can reveal some interesting truths about people if they're being honest), they need to take a drink. This game inevitably descends into more and more lewd sexual statements, if played with the right friends.

the question game

Anyone who's seen the film/play *Rosencrantz and Guildenstern are Dead* should be familiar with this one. It's best played between two people, but can easily be adapted to suit more. One person starts by asking a question (e.g. "What are we doing here?"), the next has to answer with a question ("We came here for a drink didn't we?") and so on. The first person to stumble, pause, or answer with a statement has to take a drink, and the game starts again. It's best not to allow any repetition or you'll soon end up in circles such as "Why?", "Why not?", "Why?", "Why not?"...

connections

This is an old classic. Player one says, for example, "Dog." Player two says something not associated with dogs, e.g. "Bricks." Player three then mentions a word not associated with bricks, e.g. "Priest," and so on in rapid succession. If anyone hesitates, then he/she has to drink, or if any player can prove a connection between the last two words then the last player has to drink. For example, you might challenge and say "In the film *The Exorcist*, the priest's surname was Bricks." (It wasn't, but you get the idea.)

beer pong

As drinking games go, this one is a highly aerobic form of exercise, being a booze-inspired variation on basic ping pong, so you'll need a ping pong table, paddles, and a ball–plus plenty of beer!

Each player places a large cup of beer on the center of his or her end of the table, about a paddle's length in from the edge. The goal of the game is to smack the other player's cup with the ping pong ball, while obeying the regular rules of ping pong. Each time your cup is hit, you have to drink. And to make it more interesting, if the other player knocks your cup over with a particularly powerful smash, you have to clean up the mess, get a fresh beer, and down the entire contents. You also have to down the beer if your opponent manages to land the ball in your drink. If your opponent is good, it won't be long before the room's spinning.

You can keep score and play that the first person to down 10 gulps is the loser (a good way to score if there's a line of people waiting to play), but generally a person loses when they have to drink the entire cup.

asshole

This one takes some mastering, but it's well worth the effort. Six or seven cards are dealt to each player. The cards rank from 2 (the highest), through A, K, Q, J, etc. down to 3. Someone is chosen play the first card, and the next person must play a higher card or pass on that turn. Each successive player must play a higher card. A new hand starts when all players pass, or when someone plays a 2 (the most powerful card). The last person to play a card leads the next hand. This proceeds until all players have played all their cards. The first player out of cards is the President for the next round, the next out becomes the Vice President, the next players out are normal, and the last person out is the Asshole.

If the person leading has two cards the same, this person may play them both, and then the next player must play a pair of a higher card. Three, or even four, of the same card may be led. The only time a player may lay one card instead of the number of cards played is if it is an all-powerful 2.

The roles for each player are as follows:

The President can make any player drink at any time, no one can make the President drink (except the President), the President is the first player to start each round (one of the benefits of power), and the President should never have to refill his or her own beer.

The Vice President can make any player (except the President) drink at any time, and only the President or the Vice President can make the Vice President drink. The Vice President goes second in each round.

Normal People: these players can make each other drink, as well as the Asshole. They play in the order they finished the previous round; first normal out follows the Vice President, second normal out follows the first, etc.

The Asshole is, for several reasons, truly the Asshole. This unfortunate player has to deal all the cards, clear up the cards after the hands, and cannot make any other player drink. The Asshole plays last in each round.

Here are a few recommendations. At the end of each round, the players should move seats in order to reflect the new hierachy and the proper playing order. Always play your lowest cards first. Feel free to abuse the power when you are the President or Vice President, but remember your evil deeds will eventually be repaid, especially when you abuse the Asshole. Someday they'll be President!

catchphrase

A great TV watcher's favorite, Catchphrase involves having a drink each time a character in a TV show or a film utters his or her particular catchphrase or cliché, e.g. Captain Kirk saying "Beam me up Scotty," Homer Simpson saying "Doh!" or Joe Pesci saying "F***."

A variant of this game includes the spotting of mannerisms, e.g. Giles from *Buffy* removing his spectacles thoughtfully, or Joey giving an Italianate shrug in *Friends*.

"THAT IS ILLOGICAL CAPTAIN."

If you want to be fancy, you can allocate a different drink for each catchphrase or mannerism, e.g. a gin and tonic for "That's illogical captain," a whiskey sour for "He's dead, Jim," and a bloody Mary for "She cannae take it! She's gonna blow." No doubt you can think of plenty of good film and TV examples to add to the list.

kings

This really is a cruel game, but it's hysterical to watch in the final rounds. You'll need a deck of cards, and a pitcher or big cup that's placed in the center of the table. You'll also need to agree on a definition of a "sip." The cards are spread out, face down, around the pitcher in a circle. Everyone draws a card on their turn. What you got tells you what to do.

If it's an Ace, it's a Social, and everyone drinks. If it's a 2, 3, 4, or 5, you have to take that many sips of your drink. If it's a 6, 7, 8, or 9, you choose someone at the table and they have to take that many sips. If it's a 10, then the person on your right or your left (you choose) has to take a sip.

Now for the court cards. If it's a Jack, that's Categories: you have to think of a subject area (for example, cars), but don't say what it is. You then say a brand name (for example Ferrari). Everybody follows suit and the person who doesn't get the topic or can't name something has to drink. If the card you pick up is a Queen, that's a Question. You must ask anyone in the group a question, which they must answer and they must drink as well. If the card is a King, that's the big one. The first person to pick up a King pours their beer (or whatever they're drinking) in the pitcher. The second person to pick up a King does the same. The third pours their drink in and then sets a time limit. The fourth King has to drink whatever concoction is in the pitcher in the allotted time. Good luck!

shot pool

If you want to combine a standard game of pool with an excuse to do some serious drinking, you should drink a shot of Smirnoff Red whenever you pot a red. Every time you pot a yellow it should be a shot of Cuervo Gold. If the white is accidentally potted, the one responsible should sink a Bailey's, and the one who sinks the black can choose to have a triple shot of Blavod Black Vodka bought for himself or for his opponent.

3 man

This is a game where one person (the 3 man) gets to drink a lot very quickly. Select a person to start the first roll of the two dice (preferably not you). From the beginning, the first person to roll a 3 on either die, or a total of 3 (2+1), becomes the 3 man. From this point on, anytime a 3 or a total of 3 is rolled, the 3 man has to take a single drink. If a 7 is rolled, the person to the roller's left must drink ("7-ahead"). If an 11 is rolled, the person to the roller's right must drink ("11-behind"). If doubles are rolled, the roller gets to hand out drinks (pair of 6's = 6 drinks to hand out). Players take turns rolling until the dice don't cause a drink. The 3 man only loses his position after rolling a 3. The next person to roll a 3 then becomes the 3-man.

roxanne

All you need for this one is the song *Roxanne* by The Police. Every time you hear the words "Roxanne" or "red light" in the song, everyone has to drink. Sounds too easy? They say "Roxanne" a lot in this song!

captain bluff

This is a manically fast-moving game and can be great fun with the right crowd. The nominated player starts by saying "Captain Bluff takes his first drink of the evening." On saying this, the player picks up his drink with thumb and one finger, takes one sip, puts it down tapping it once on the table, taps his right shoulder with one finger of his left hand, taps his left shoulder with one finger from his right hand, taps his right shoulder with one finger of his right hand, and finally taps his left shoulder with one finger from his left hand. Once all players have succeeded in doing this, they move on to Captain Bluff's "second drink of the evening" using two of everything and tapping twice, and then his third, and so on. Any mistakes incur the inevitable drinking forfeits, increasing the chances of more mistakes!

synonyms

for being drunk

befuddled	drunk-as-a-skunk	pickled
bent	euphoric	pie-eyed
blacked-out	fried	pissed (as a newt)
bladdered	giddy	plastered
blasted	groggy	plowed
blind	hammered	plotzed
blitzed	high	polluted
blotto	hooched-up	pot-valiant
boiled-as-an-owl	hung-one-on	ripped
bombed	inebriated	roaring
buttered	in one's cups	sauced
canned	intoxicated	shickered
clobbered	juiced	shit-faced
cockeyed	legless	slopped-up
crapulous	liquored-up	sloshed
crocked	loaded	smashed
cut	looped	snockered
destroyed	mellow	sodden
dipso	obliterated	soused
		sozzled
		spaced
		stewed

synonyms

a drink by any other name...

stiff	amber nectar	mountain dew
stinking	aqua vitae	neck oil
stinko	bevie	nip
stoned	bib	pledge
swacked	booze	poison
tanked	brewski	ruddy cup
tied-one-on	cold one	sauce
three-sheets-to-the-wind	cup	singing syrup
tight	demon drink	souse
tipsy	extra	sup
toasted	firewater	swill
tweaked	flowing bowl	tank up
twisted	frosty	tinny
under-the-influence	grog	tipple
under-the-table	hooch	toast
under-the-weather	inebriant	tot
wasted	intoxicant	tube
wiped-out	John Barleycorn	water of life
woozy	liquor	wee dram
wrecked		
zoned		
zonked		

glossary of terms

LIKE MOST IMPORTANT ASPECTS OF CULTURE, THE PREPARATION AND CONSUMPTION OF ALCOHOL HAVE A LANGUAGE ALL OF THEIR OWN. HERE ARE SOME KEYS TO THE MYSTERY.

AGAVE The family of plants used to produce mescal and tequila.

ANGOSTURA An aromatic bitter bark.

APERITIF A drink taken before a meal as an appetizer. Champagne can be served as an aperitif, as can Campari or vermouth.

APPLEJACK US brandy distilled from cider.

ARMAGNAC Brandy from the French province of Gascony.

BOTANICALS Herbs used in winemaking or distillation.

BRANDY SNIFTER The classic blown-glass globular shaped brandy glass designed with a brief stem to allow the hand to warm the brandy.

CHASER An alcoholic drink that is consumed immediately after another that is either weaker or stronger, e.g. a shot of whiskey followed by a beer chaser, or a vodka after a Guinness.

DIGESTIF A drink taken after a meal to aid digestion (any excuse, eh?).

DISTILLATION The method of making a spirit through heating a liquid up to the temperature at which the alcohol evaporates, and then cooling the vapor so that the alcohol condenses.

EGGNOG A traditional Christmas drink made of brandy, rum, or bourbon with eggs, sugar, cream or milk, and served cold.

FRAPPÉ Anything served with finely crushed ice.

GROG A kind of drink made with a rum base, fruit, and various sweeteners, and served either hot or cold in a large mug or glass.

HIGHBALL Any spirit served with ice and club soda in a medium to tall glass.

LOWBALL Any spirit served with ice alone, or with water or soda in a short glass.

MALT A whiskey whose raw material is only malt barley.

MULLS Any wine or ale that has been warmed, spiced, and sweetened.

NEAT Of any spirit, drunk straight, without the addition of ice or a mixer.

NIGHTCAP Any drink that is taken immediately before going to bed. Favorites include milk punches, toddies, and short drinks such as liqueurs or fortified wines.

ON-THE-ROCKS Any wine or spirit poured over ice cubes, usually in an Old Fashioned glass.

PICK-ME-UP Any drink designed to alleviate the effects of overindulgence of drinking, i.e. to stave off, or reduce the severity of, a hangover.

PUNCH A combination of spirits, wine, sweeteners, flavorings, and fruit garnishes, mixed together and served in a large bowl.

SHOOTER A straight shot of whiskey or other kind of spirit taken neat.

SHOT GLASS The original bar measure, holding up to to two ounces.

THUJONE The active ingredient found in absinthe, and said to account for its hallucinatory properties.

TODDY A combination of spirits, sugar, spices, and lemon peel mixed with hot water.

TOT A small amount of any spirit.

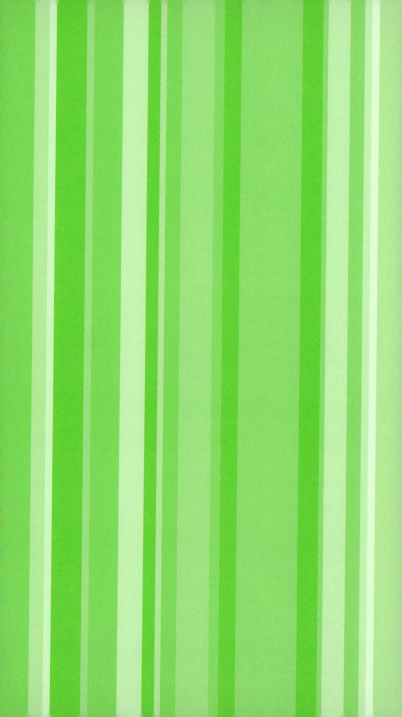